D1285237

A New Library of
the Supernatural

Healing Without Medicine

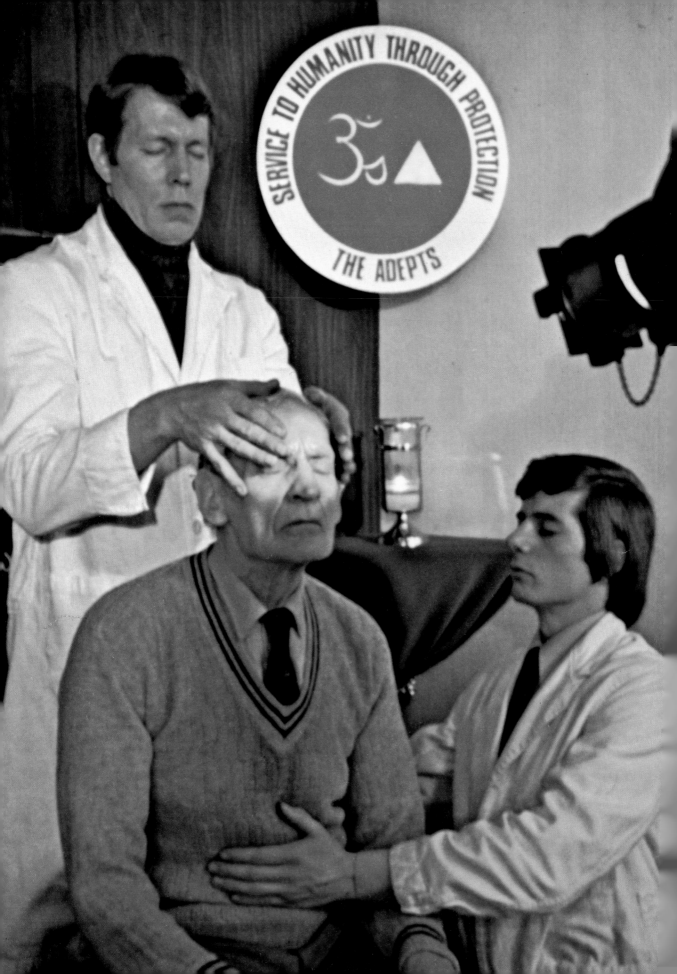

SERVICE TO HUMANITY THROUGH PROTECTION

THE ADEPTS

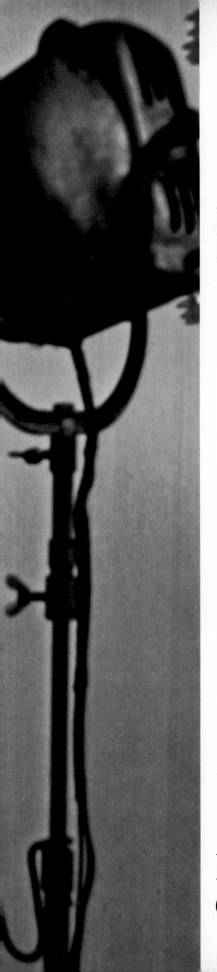

Healing Without Medicine

by Jeremy Kingston

Doubleday and Company, Inc.
Garden City, New York, 1976

EDITORIAL CONSULTANTS:

COLIN WILSON
DR. CHRISTOPHER EVANS

Series Coordinator: John Mason
Design Director: Günter Radtke
Picture Editor: Peter Cook
Editor: Sally Burningham
Copy Editor: Mitzi Bales
Research: Sarah Waters
General Consultant: Beppie Harrison

Library of Congress Cataloging in Publication Data
Kingston, Jeremy
Healing Without Medicine
(A New Library of the Supernatural; v. 9)
1. Mental Healing   2. Medicine, Magic,
Mystic, and Spagiric   3. Therapeutic Systems
I. Title   II. Series
RZ400.K56   615'.85   75-34860
ISBN 0-385-11319-6

Doubleday and Company
ISBN: 0-385-11319-6

Library of Congress Catalog
Card No. 75-34860

A New Library of the Supernatural
ISBN: 11327-7

© 1976 Aldus Books Limited, London

Printed and bound in Italy by
Amilcare Pizzi S.p.A.
Cinisello Balsamo (Milano)

**Frontispiece: an Aetherius Society healing session.
Above: Pazuzu, an Assyrian demon who caused fevers.**

Healing Without Medicine

Today, with all the accumulated wisdom of Western medicine, many people still look to unorthodox means of getting and staying healthy. Acupuncture, osteopathy and chiropractic, spiritual healing and psychic surgery, and radionics — here is a look at alternative medicine in the modern world.

Contents

1

Borderland of Medicine

In April 1974 a middle-aged Englishman, vacationing in the attractive North Italian town of Lucca, stretched himself out on his hotel bed. It so happened that the springy mattress had not been properly settled into the framework, and during the night he was abruptly ejected onto the hard tile floor with the mattress on top of him. The man was Ian Parsons, chairman of a London publishing firm. As a result of this accident Parsons developed severe pain in his shoulder and left arm, and a continual sensation of pins and needles in his left hand. On his return to England he tried drugs, physiotherapy, osteopathy, massage, traction, and injections

Few people today suffer pain willingly. When orthodox medicine fails to bring relief, increasing numbers of people turn to the alternative healing arts to seek some therapy that will cure their own particular affliction. Right: actor Lorne Greene went through orthodox treatment before he turned to acupuncture to find relief for his persistent back pain. After his first treatment, the pain vanished completely.

"Acupuncture... a healing method that cures the body by sticking needles into it"

to cure the pain. Some of the treatments made his condition worse; none improved it. Finally he went to a nearby town to see an acupuncturist, a Chinese whose father and grandfather had followed the same calling before him. The practitioner inserted a number of fine silver needles into various parts of Parson's body. Such treatment was maintained for 12 sessions.

"Nothing happened after the first two or three visits," Parsons explained. "Then, after the third the 'fizzing' in my left hand went. After each subsequent visit the extent of the pain receded up the arm to the shoulder, and across the back, until at last it was gone."

Did acupuncture cure Parsons? This question must be asked, for in cases cured by any form of treatment the possibility always exists that the trouble might have cleared up anyway. But Parsons's case has a significant epilogue. A month after his twelfth visit the pain reappeared in the shoulder, and to a lesser degree in the upper arm. He told the acupuncturist about his shoulder and a further treatment cured the pain there. But he forgot to mention the pain in his arm. A final treatment finally cured that once and for all. The separate cure of these two attacks of *returned* pain convincingly identifies the healing with the acupuncture.

A healing method that cures the body by sticking needles into it sounds strange to those accustomed to Western medical treatment. Yet acupuncture has been practiced successfully in China for over 5000 years. Its origins can be traced to the Stone Age when it was probably believed that the insertion of needles enabled pent up and harmful forces in the body to be released. The discovery that needles inserted at certain points helped to cure specific pains gradually followed, and after centuries of experience the complex theory of acupuncture was developed. This theory was expressed in terms of the Chinese Taoist philosophy which states that everything in the Universe is composed of the two complementary forces of Yang and Yin. Yang is the active, positive, outgoing element, and Yin is the passive, negative, soft element. Yang is also said to represent light and Yin dark. Both are equally essential and together they make up the life force known as Ch'i. When Yang and Yin are balanced the result is harmony, but excess of one or the other in a person leads to illness.

The principle authority on how to practice acupuncture is a semimystical textbook over 2000 years old. It is called *The Yellow Emperor's Book of Internal Medicine,* and it is written in the form of a dialogue between two legendary figures from China's past—the physician Ch'i Po and the emperor Huang Ti. In the extract below the emperor is warned of the danger of an excess of Yang in the body:

"When Yang is stronger the body is hot, the pores are closed and the people begin to pant; they become boisterous and coarse and whether one looks up or down no perspiration appears. People become feverish, their gums are dry and give trouble, the stomach is oppressed and people die of constipation. When Yang is stronger people can endure Winter but they cannot endure Summer."

The purpose of acupuncture is to restore the balance of Yin

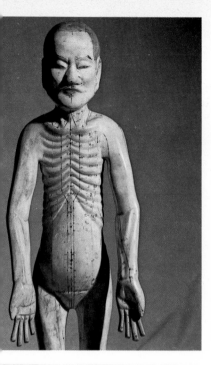

and Yang in the life force Ch'i. The life force is said to flow through the body along various channels known as meridians. These meridians do not correspond either to the circulatory or nervous systems. In fact, despite their essential role in acupuncture, their existence has never been conclusively proved. But their routes around the body have been carefully mapped on detailed charts and models. Twelve are associated with a particular internal organ, and are referred to by that organ's name, such as the heart meridian, the gall bladder meridian and so forth. The remainder are minor branch and connecting meridians.

Positioned along these meridians like stations on an intricate railroad system are the points at which the acupuncturist's

Left: Tsoë-Bosi, a model used for teaching the techniques of the ancient art of acupuncture. This Chinese method of treatment was in use over 2000 years before the Christian era, and has a long and respected history in the Far East as well as many practitioners.

Below: television actor Lyle Waggoner taking acupuncture treatment for backache. Today more and more Westerners are turning to this Eastern science for relief from many kinds of illnesses and pains.

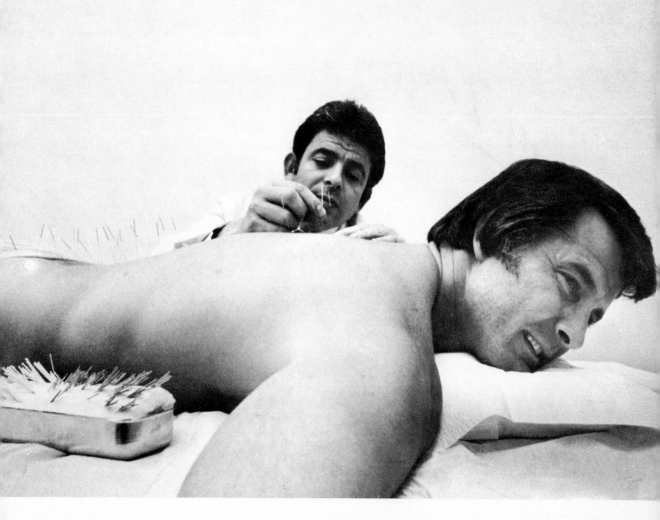

Left: Yin and Yang, the symbols of opposite energy forces so important to Chinese philosophy, also have a meaning in acupuncture. Health, it is said, is a balance of Yin and Yang within the body, and an excess of one or the other force leads to illness.

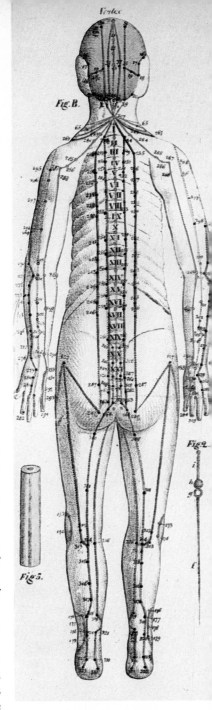

Above: the meridian lines of acupuncture from a French text of about 1850. Acupuncture was first introduced to the West in the 17th century by Jesuit missionaries who had been sent to Peking. There are bilateral meridians having identical branches on each side of the body, unilateral meridians that pass through the midline of the body, and extraordinary meridians that are diversionary channels through which excess energy flows.

needles can be inserted. In a healthy person these may be difficult to find, but in a sick person the relevant meridian is said to be activated, and the points reveal themselves as painful or even as slightly hard areas about 2mm in diameter. About 950 points have been identified.

The presence of these points along the meridians explains why remote parts of the body influence each other. When a needle is inserted and twirled in the big toe—the start of the spleen meridian—the effect can be felt along the other 20 points of that meridian. These go up the leg and across the hip, abdomen, and chest to the armpit. Some meridians contain only a few points. For example, the heart meridian contains only nine. But as many as 67 points occur from top to toe of the body on the important bladder meridian.

The experience of centuries has shown that certain points are especially influential. Some can be used to increase the energy passing along a meridian; others to reduce an excess. Every meridian contains one point at which a needle can give quick relief from pain. Other points are associated with the cure of specific ailments. Illnesses caused by external agents such as climate, infection, and contagion, are said to be the effect of excess Yang. Internal troubles originate from too much Yin. Traumatic and accidental injuries, including war wounds, are considered to come from an imbalance of both Yin and Yang. There are Yin organs and Yang organs, dominant organs, and other interrelations of organs, all of which the acupuncturist takes into account in forming a diagnosis. If the problem is gastro-intestinal, the practitioner may decide to insert the needle at the second point on the large intestine meridian, near the base of the index finger.

Accurate diagnosis is the key to success in acupuncture, and much more reliance than in Western medicine is placed on reading the pulse. Each of the 12 meridians has its own pulse. The acupuncturist will assess them in turn, first at the wrist, then at the neck and elsewhere, gauging not only the rate but also many other characteristics. Each of the 12 pulses may have any one of the 27 qualities on which acupuncturists' diagnoses depend. Their skill is so great that they not only can describe the patient's present condition, but also list past illnesses and predict future ones. Dr. Felix Mann, President of the British Acupuncture Society, refers to "the taut, wiry pulse of pain;

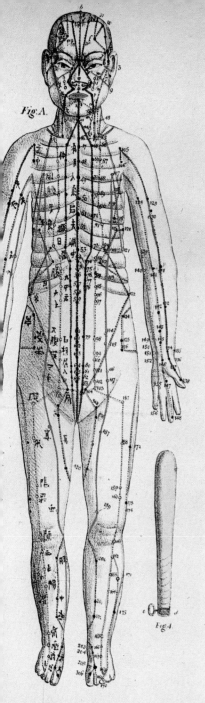

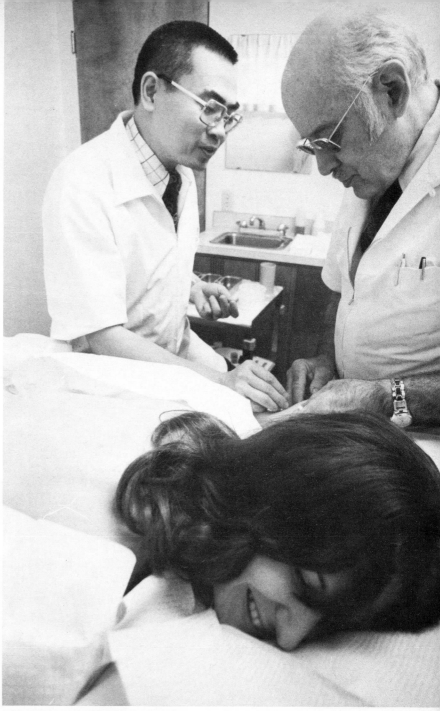

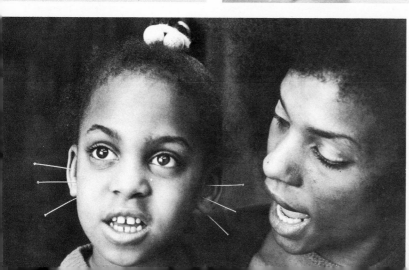

Above: acupuncturist Kim Lai administering a backache cure at a clinic in Seattle, Washington. The problem of incorporating non-doctors such as acupuncturists into American medical practice has been treated differently in various states. In Washington the solution has been for the non-physician to practice only under direct supervision of a doctor. Left: a five-year-old girl being treated by acupuncture for her condition of nerve deafness.

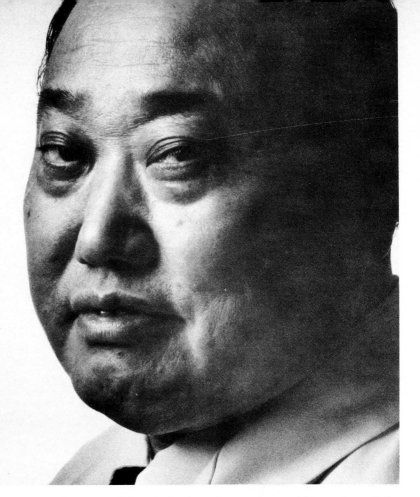

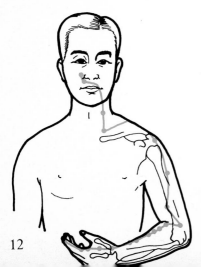

Above: Dr. Ling Sung Chu, a New York physician who received his medical training in China and Germany. He holds the acupuncture needles he used to treat Governor George Wallace for the paralysis resulting from the attempt on his life in 1972. Below: the meridian for the large intestine. Like other bilateral meridians, this one has altogether 20 points—10 on each side of the body—which show increased sensitivity in cases of illness.

the hollow pulse of loss of Yin energy; the pecking pulse of the erratic; the full pulse of congestion; the flitting smooth pulse of the hypersensitive, etc." In the ancient book Ch'i Po tells the Yellow Emperor:

"The pulse of the liver should sound like the strings of a musical instrument; the pulse of the heart should sound like the blows of a hammer; the pulse of the spleen should be intermittent and irregular; the pulse of the lungs should be soft like hair and feathers; the pulse of the kidneys should sound like a stone. . . ."

Many Western doctors refuse to believe that pulses can possess so many distinct qualities. But though it seems almost incredible, skilled acupuncturists can locate a patient's weakness or ailment by pulse diagnosis alone. Generally they will also examine the color of the patient's skin, ask questions about his or her way of life, and take into account the time of year, time of day, and certain other semimystical factors. They then know from their training the precise nature of the Yang-Yin disturbance that has occurred, and which points must be activated, how deeply and how long.

After centuries of practice acupuncture fell into disfavor in the period before World War II, and Western medicine was introduced wherever possible. With the Communist revolution of 1949, however, acupuncture was again regarded with respect, and Mao Tse Tung ordered that it be taught in medical schools together with Western medicine. Acupuncturists thereafter successfully treated patients for asthma, bronchitis, convulsions, dysentery, emphysema, fevers, gastritis, haemorrhoids, and scores of other ailments both emotional and physical. They worked alongside doctors practicing Western medicine, and in surgical cases the methods of East and West were sometimes brought together, the acupuncturist's needles being used instead of an anesthetic.

Astonishingly, sometimes the insertion of a single needle is enough to produce anesthesia. In 1971 Dr. E. Gray Dimond, at that time Chairman of the Health Sciences Department at the University of Missouri Medical School, visited China in the company of three other leading American men of medicine. They went to hospitals both in large cities and remote rural communes, and among the operations they witnessed were ten in which acupuncture was the only anesthetic used. In one of these, the patient underwent an operation to remove his lung. One steel needle was inserted and twirled at a point on his left arm. Still awake and alert but feeling no pain, he was able to have the surgeon cut into his chest and begin removing the top half of his left lung.

In October 1971 the *AMA News*, published by the American Medical Association, records Dr. Dimond's observations as follows: "The patient's chest was wide open. I could see his heart beating, and all this time the man continued to talk to us cheerfully with total coherence. Halfway through the operation he said he was hungry so the doctors stopped working and gave him a can of fruit to eat."

In the same year of 1971 James Reston, distinguished columnist of the *New York Times*, became the first American to be treated by acupuncture in Communist China. It came about when he was struck down by an acute attack of appendicitis during a tour of Peking. After the necessary operation in which Western anesthetic was used, he had the fairly common reaction of severe stomach cramps. On being asked if he would accept acupuncture treatment, he agreed. The acupuncturist duly arrived and inserted one needle into Reston's elbow and two others into his lower legs, twirling them for a period of 20 minutes. Then he burned a herbal powder in front of Reston's stomach. The pain stopped.

The Chinese have never been greatly concerned to know why acupuncture works. They are content that it does. But recent research outside China has led to discoveries that could bring this ancient art of healing a little way out of the strange realm of the unexplained. Several groups of doctors in Russia, for example, have found that acupuncture points differ from the surrounding skin in temperature and in electrical potential. The points also produce less noise when rubbed by a sensitive stethoscope. A Korean doctor, Professor Kim Bong-Han, has published his discovery that variations in the skin's electrical resistance can even be traced along the paths of the meridians. The means by which acupuncture works may still be invisible but they no longer go undetected.

Another suggestion has been that the action of the needles might stimulate the production of antibodies which then set to work to fight infection. Dr. G. M. Bull of London has advanced still another theory to explain how acupuncture could produce

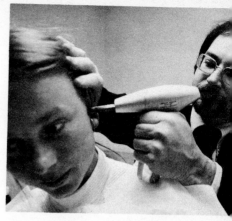

Above and below: inserting wire staples in the ear is a method of curing drug addiction developed by Dr. Lester Sacks of Los Angeles. He adapted the idea from Hong Kong acupuncturists who treat addiction with electrically charged needles in the ear. The staple is not noticed until wiggled or tapped. When so touched it gives the drug addict, heavy smoker, or compulsive eater a shock which somehow interferes with his or her strong craving.

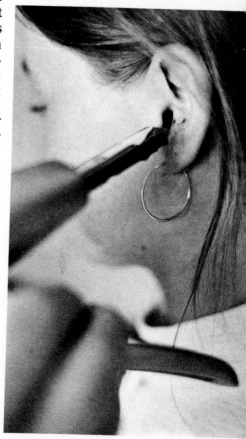

local anesthesia. He points out that an increase of stimulation in one area of the nervous system can frequently "deafen" the cortex of the brain to stimuli from elsewhere. In 1973 he suggested that the essentially rhythmic vibration that results from the twirling of the needles could be a crucial factor in the treatment. Applied to the operation witnessed by Dr. Dimond in China, this would mean that the vibration of the needle in the patient's arm caused a large area of the cortex to be "locked on" to that frequency. This area would then be unable to receive the stimuli it ordinarily received from the organs being cut into— the chest and lungs in this case.

Much research remains to be done but acupuncture is not like some newly discovered drug to be tested and retested in the laboratory thousands of times before being offered to the public. The Chinese have tested acupuncture in practice a billion times, and many millions in China today rely confidently upon it. A much smaller, though increasing, number of people outside China do the same. Acupuncture still has powerful opponents, notably in America. Among them are drug manufacturers unlikely to view with favor a discipline that places no reliance on drugs, but relies instead on no more sophisticated aids than a box of fine needles, a selection of herbs, and a high degree of skill.

Many people have become disillusioned with the impersonalisation of much orthodox medicine. Many have also realized that there are methods of healing that orthodox practitioners cannot perform satisfactorily, or have not been trained to perform at all. Medical students are taught the structure of bones, and learn the diseases that attack bone; but their knowledge of how to manipulate bones to restore their smooth working is limited. Not only that. For a long time teachers at medical schools opposed the work of the men who did know bone manipulation. Chiropractors and osteopaths were forced to endure long years of abuse in the struggle to establish themselves as honorable professionals. In the United States chiropractors were imprisoned on charges of practicing medicine without a license, while in Britain any doctor who worked in association with an osteopath ran the risk of being struck off the medical register. In 1911 the British Medical Association struck off Dr. Frederick Axham for acting as anesthetist to Herbert Barker, the most distinguished "manipulative surgeon" of his day. Barker later was knighted by King George V for his successful treatment of soldiers during World War I, but he was never accepted by the medical profession. Nor was Axham's name ever restored to the register. Even today good relations between doctors on the one hand and chiropractors and osteopaths on the other frequently have to be maintained on an unofficial basis.

Throughout the ages there have been people who possessed a knack for pressing a dislocated bone back into place, as chiropractors and osteopaths do. Gifted with exceptionally sensitive fingers, their skill at bonesetting was often a part-time occupation, separate from their day-to-day work. Some bonesetters became famous. In 18th-century London one of the most formidable was Mrs. Sarah Mapp, a no-nonsense woman who counted the Queen of England among her clients. She showed a

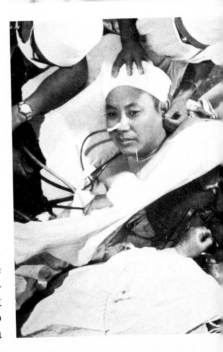

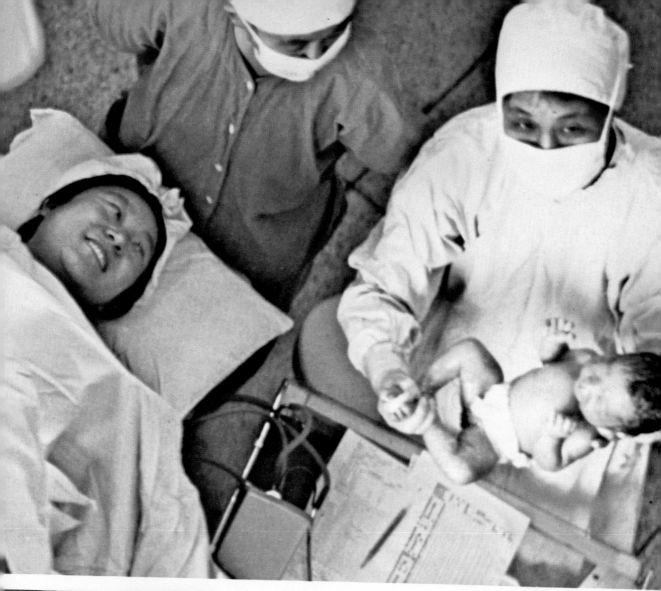

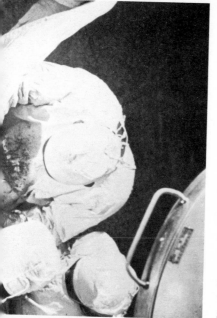

Above: a Chinese woman has a baby delivered by a Caesarian section operation with acupuncture as her only anesthesia. Acupuncture as anesthetic leaves patients fully conscious but entirely pain-free.
Left: under acupuncture, a tumor is removed from the esophagus.

devilish sense of humor when faced with critics or doubters. She was once asked to cure a man who was in fact perfectly well, but had been instructed by some envious doctors to complain of a dislocation. The plan was to expose her to ridicule once she claimed to have put the dislocation right. Sarah Mapp was shrewd enough to guess the plot, and turned it upside down by dislocating the unfortunate man's shoulder on purpose. She then sent him back to the doctors with a message that if they couldn't put it right she would do so on his return to her.

By the end of the 19th century bonesetting had evolved into the twin skills of osteopathy and chiropractic. To an outsider there may not seem much difference between these two healing arts. Both believe that illness is caused when faults develop in the body's mechanical structure—the muscles and the bones— and that if such faults are corrected the body will recover its

15

Left: in medieval times, setting a bone was an ordeal for patient and doctor alike. This woodcut from a 1579 French text shows "the first manner of putting a Shoulder into joint." The text stresses that the arm must be placed in a sling, "lest the bone newly set, may fall out again."

good health. At one time there was a difference in opinion as to how these structural faults affected the rest of the body. Osteopaths believed that a displaced joint pinched a capillary vessel and interfered with normal blood circulation. Chiropractors on the other hand claimed that a displaced joint affected a nerve. Nowadays they agree that circulatory and neural systems are both likely to suffer. In practice, the most significant difference between them is that a chiropractor will be more likely to reposition a bone by means of a firm thrust, whereas an osteopath will apply the principles of leverage.

Osteopathy was founded by Andrew Taylor Still, the son of a Methodist preacher in Virginia. In 1864 three of his children developed spinal meningitis. Drugs could not save them, and all three died. As Still looked down on the bodies of his dead children he dedicated himself to finding a remedy for others struck down by disease.

He no longer believed in the power of drugs. Gradually he became convinced that the answer to the body's ills lay within the body itself. He wrote in his *Autobiography*: "So wise a God had certainly placed the remedy within the material home in which the spirit of life dwells."

For 10 years Still studied human anatomy. He dug up bodies from their graves to dissect them, and he carried bones around with him in his pockets so as to be able to feel them and consider how they worked at any time of the day. Finally he came to the conclusion that ill-health was caused by spinal lesions— injuries that interfered with the normal movement of the joints but which were sometimes so slight that the patient remained unaware of them. He said of his conclusion: "I took the position in 1874 that the living blood swarmed with health corpuscles which were carried to all parts of the body. Interfere with that current of blood and you steam down the river of life and land in the ocean of death."

Like acupuncturists, Still believed in a life force. He gave it no special name. He just believed it had to be kept flowing properly. Like acupuncturists too he formed his diagnoses by carefully examining the body with his fingers. An acupuncturist feels variations in pulses. Still and the osteopaths who followed his teaching felt the spine for tiny variations in position. They believed that manipulation of the spine would allow the life-giving current of blood and the life force to flow freely again.

Below: an early manipulator, Nicholas André, demonstrates the method by which a slanting neck can be adjusted in a young patient. He was one of the earliest medical men to recognize that abnormalities could be more easily dealt with when the patient was still very young.

ET PLURIMA MORTIS IMAGO

Left: this 18th-century caricature by Hogarth shows Sarah Mapp, the famous bonesetter, in the middle of the top row. Hogarth called it *The Undertaker's Arms, or a Consultation of Physicians,* and described the lower group as "twelve quack heads." Sarah Mapp was no stranger to mockery and jeering, which she did not hesitate to return in full part.

Below: Sir Herbert Barker, a leading British specialist in manipulative surgery. He was originally intended by his family for the legal profession, but he showed early that he had a great manipulative ability, and preferred to study osteopathy.

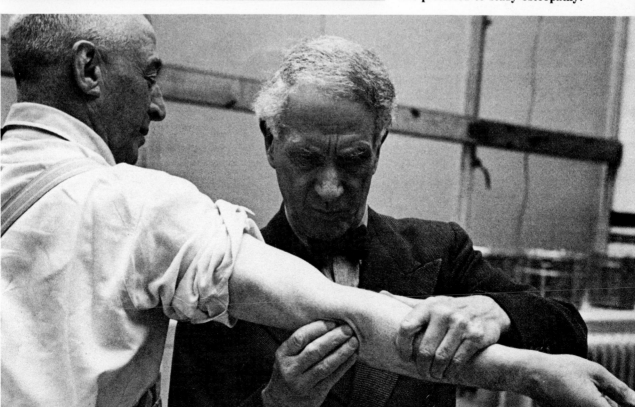

Above: Andrew Taylor Still, the founder of osteopathy. He was born in 1828, and spent his early career in politics before devoting himself to a search for a method of healing without drugs.

The early osteopaths made no use of drugs, and in the first enthusiasm for their technique believed it could cure almost every affliction. Still's maxim was, "Find it, fix it, and leave it alone." Osteopaths no longer regard their system as a complete system of healing, but consider the field in which it can be successful as extremely broad. Maladies caused by mechanical faults and bone disturbance—dislocations, sprains, slipped cartilages, backaches, and other mysterious aches of uncertain location—have often been cured by osteopaths when medical doctors have declared themselves unable to help.

Chiropractic began as a miracle cure. The man who performed it was Daniel David Palmer, a middle-aged man who already practiced magnetic healing. In 1895 he overheard the janitor of his office explaining how he had become deaf. Seventeen years before, the man said, he had bent over and felt something "go" in his back. Palmer examined his back and discovered a lump in the neck. It was a vertebra out of place. He stood the deaf man in a doorway so that the wooden surround made a firm headrest, and with the side of his hand thrust against the vertebra. There was a loud click—and the janitor's hearing returned at once.

Palmer's background would hardly impress the doctors of his day. He was medically unqualified and he practiced a kind of quack healing part luck, part misunderstood science, and part mumbo-jumbo. But there was a fourth part the doctors ignored —and in many cases continue to ignore to this day—and that was intuition. Palmer's hands could sense what to do with the janitor's neck. The system of healing he founded was named from the Greek *kheir*, hand, and *praktike*, efficient. He freely translated it as "done by hand," and though he tried to explain in scientific terms how his system worked, he found—as Andrew Still had before him—that it was impossible to do so. Science and anatomical knowledge are insufficient to describe precisely how bonesetting and its various allied skills actually work. Still's methods were more intuitive than he realized—and his powers of suggestion and ability to inspire confidence in his patients were also greater than he took credit for. Sir Herbert Barker described what he felt when he examined the dislocated elbow of his first patient in these words:

"I thrilled as I took hold of the injured member, whilst something seemed to guide my hand and regulate the strength of my movements as—almost tenderly—I ran my tingling fingers over a prominence which I thought ought not to be there. Then I, trusting to an instinctive guidance and using my common sense, executed what I deemed was the necessary hold and leverage and, in a trice, something 'gave' and the arm resumed its normal shape."

This instinctive sense is basic to every chiropractor and osteopath—and to practitioners of many other varieties of unorthodox healing. Training in technique is necessary to put intuition to the best use, but fundamentally that intuition can be demonstrated but not explained.

Yet, if the majority of orthodox doctors could have had their way, as recently as a generation ago Still, Palmer, and their successors would have been branded as dangerous quacks.

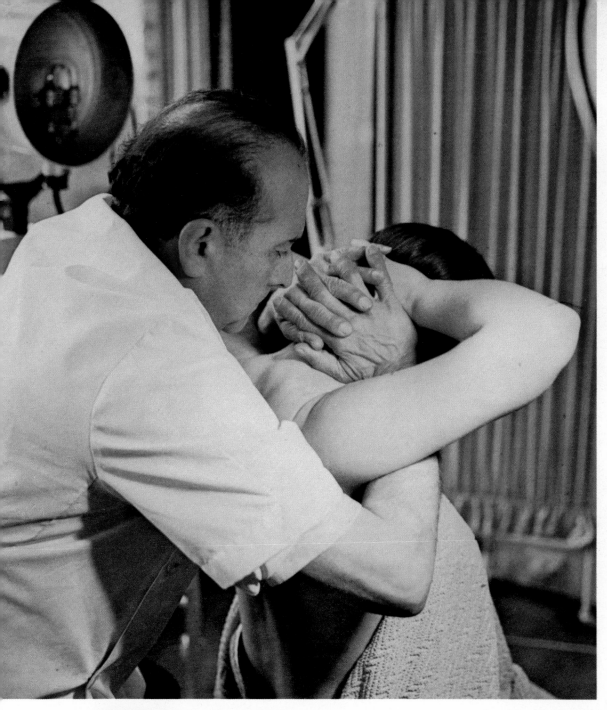

Above: an osteopath at work. In this case he is manipulating the cervical region of his patient's spine to relieve painful tension of the muscles of the neck.

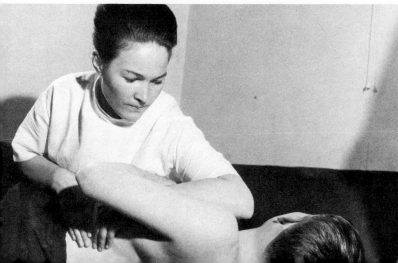

Left: osteopathic manipulation of the lower back. Pain in the lower back is the most frequent single symptom encountered in the average osteopathic practice.

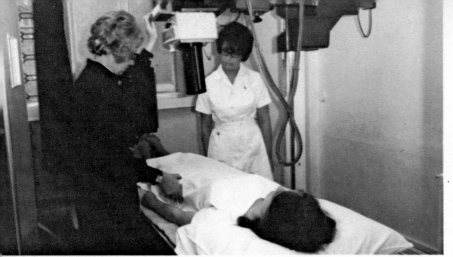

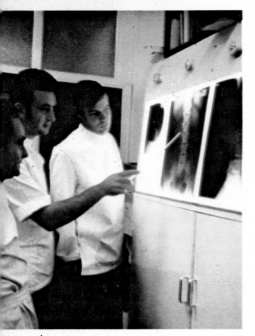

Training for osteopaths at this large school in London shows that modern osteopathy is still based on a thorough knowledge of human anatomy, but uses conventional methods of diagnosis like the X-ray. Students are taught to use them to supplement and amplify a physical examination. The early osteopaths were often highly intuitive healers, but although a natural feeling for manipulation is obviously a necessity for a student, the techniques of osteopathy are a science that can be taught. The osteopathic student studies the human body until his fingers seem to know instinctively when his patient is normal, or when there is something that will require his treatment.

Doctors often state their concern to protect the public against cynical or self-deluded healers who at best achieve nothing for a patient, and at worst leave him sicker than before. But this concern sometimes looks like crudely disguised anxiety to guard their own self-interest.

The victories of orthodox medicine over many diseases and ailments have been of undoubted value. In the course of its history, however, medicine has advanced, retreated, petrified, advanced again, petrified again, and several times lost its way among a welter of conflicting schools—each one claiming to be the sole possessor of the truth. During these twists and turns doctors have tried many remedies that were plainly foolish and others that were downright dangerous, such as the widespread 18th-century cure-all of taking blood from the sick no matter what the illness. They rejected much that was useless, but they also discarded or ignored a great deal that was beneficial.

More and more people are coming to believe that a medical doctor cannot claim a monopoly of knowledge nor consider himself the only person fit to cure the sick. There are arts—skilled arts—of healing without medicine.

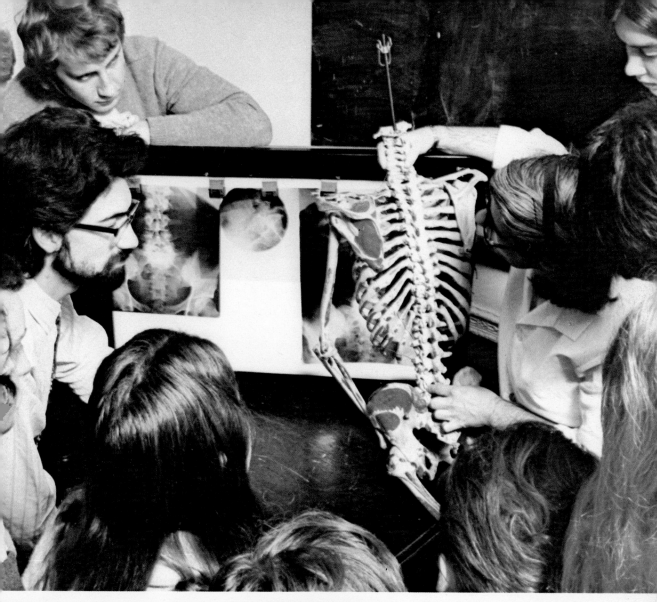

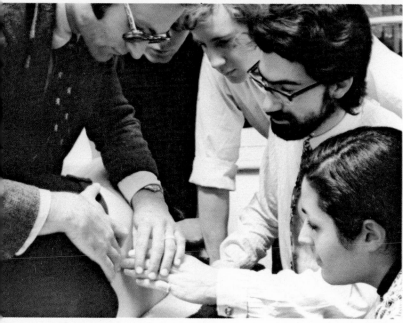

Left: anatomy turned into living terms. Clinical osteopathy can only be taught in small groups— the student's hand has to be guided again and again to teach him to feel and to interpret.

2

The Days of Magic

How far has man come from the Stone Age? In many respects the answer is a long long way. In others we are closer to it than we sometimes think. A look at how illness has been treated in the past will show how we resemble our distant ancestors.

Our prehistoric ancestors lived in a world filled with strange and powerful forces beyond their understanding: the movement of the heavenly bodies, the ebb and flow of the tides, the invisible wind, floods, storms, and most frightening of all, earthquakes and eclipses that blotted out the sun and moon. People came to associate these forces with spirits, gods, and demons—beings whose

Since mankind has existed there has been illness—and healing techniques for trying to cure it. Disease and injuries are often frightening, and an obvious primitive medical technique is to try to vanquish the disease by frightening it in return. This fearsome mask, worn by devil dancers of Sri Lanka, is to help those suffering from catarrh—a persistently runny nose.

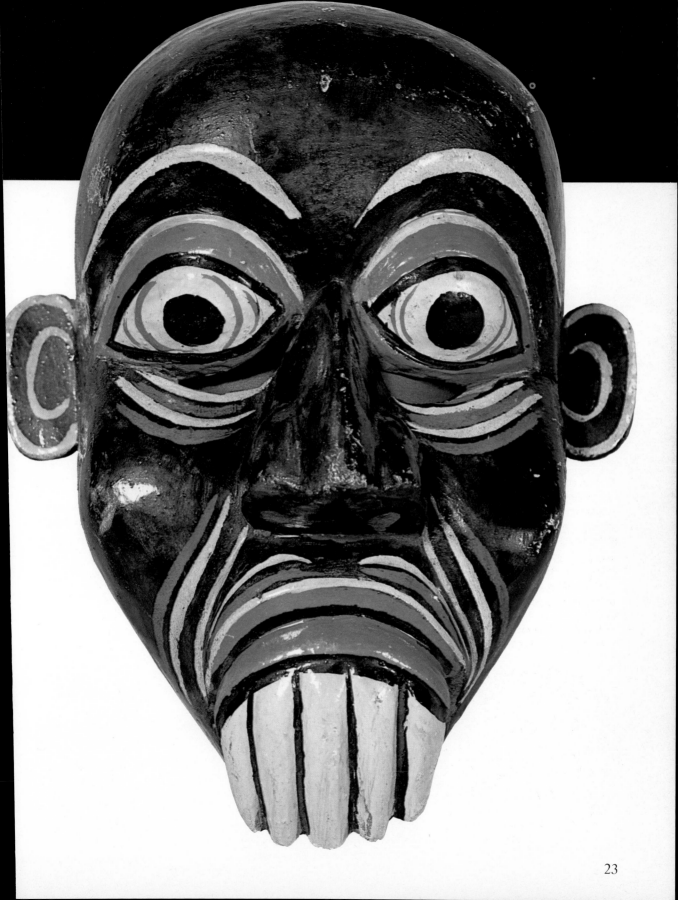

"It was natural to consider illness the work of spirits"

desires and feelings resembled their own, but who were infinitely more powerful. Everything was thought to have its own spirit—animals, trees, rivers, mountains—and early peoples devoted much energy to rituals designed to turn aside the anger of these spirits, and to persuade them to work on behalf of humans.

When someone got sick it was natural to consider his illness the work of spirits. Perhaps the person had trespassed on land sacred to the spirit of the mountain, or had forgotten to protect himself against the jealous attention of some ever-watchful demon. Perhaps another member of the tribe wished to injure him and had secured the aid of demons to strike him down. Whatever the cause, the person who had the power to cure him was the tribe's *shaman* or medicine man.

Since the source of illness was believed to be supernatural, the medicine man had to be both physician and priest. In fact, the two roles were inseparable. He performed magic to bring rain and to cure a fever; his spells could ensure the fertility of fields as well as drive out a spirit that had taken possession of a person's body. Because magical practices throughout the world are basically similar, it is possible to form a good idea of some of the methods employed by our prehistoric ancestors by studying the

Right: a Siberian shaman, who treats his patient by driving the disease-bearing evil spirits away from him into the horse.

Below: this skull dating from between 100 B.C. and A.D. 100 bears unmistakable evidence of two trephining operations in which a piece of bone was cut out. Such an operation was usually performed by a shaman to let evil spirits, including those causing sickness, escape from a person's body. Judging by the scar healing, one of these operations must have been carried out with success.

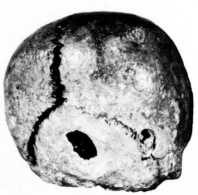

customs of primitive communities that have survived into the 20th century.

Dressed in the skins of wild animals, the shaman looked considerably like an enormous animal rearing up on its hind legs. He would advance on the sick patient, leaping and waving his arms, shouting, slapping his legs, shaking sticks or a rattle, and beating his drum. This loud racket was designed to frighten the demon and make him loose his hold on the sick person. Sometimes the medicine man would try to extract the pain from the patient's body by sucking it through a tube of bone or hollow reed and spitting it out. He sprinkled water over or blew smoke across the sufferer. He also made use of herbal remedies by placing leaves, roots, berries, or strips of bark on the patient's body to reduce fever or relieve pain. At the end of the ceremony, the shaman gave the patient an amulet to wear as a guard against further attacks from the spirits.

The natural defense weapons of animals such as teeth, claws, and horns were frequently selected as amulets. Other popular objects included jewels and bright stones, believed to be able to gather into themselves and neutralize the power of the evil eye. Cowrie shells, symbol of the female genitalia, were thought to combat harmful spirits of destruction with forces of creation.

Below: traditional treatment for a headache by a Mangyan tribesman of the Philippine Islands. He is using a *mutya*—a special stone that is believed to house a spirit.

Right: the dance of the Clallam Indian medicine men of Vancouver Island, Canada, painted by Paul Kane in 1847. These medicine men would have had considerable knowledge of herbal remedies, and in their apparently primitive chanting and dancing often took greater note of the psychological background of illness than the educated doctors of civilization were to do for many years to come.

Above: an American Indian "soul-catcher" used by shamans to bring back the soul of a sick person. It was believed that illness occurred when the soul was coaxed out of the body by some form of magic. The patient could only be returned to health when the shaman caught the soul with the catcher, and brought it back to the body it belonged to. The shaman would wear the soul catcher around his neck, suspended on bright beads.

The medicine man might decide his patient needed greater protection than an amulet could provide. In such a case he selected an object and implanted a spirit in it. This kind of protection is known as a fetish. Besides guarding its owner, a fetish is capable of harming others. If one is buried at the entrance of a hut it will cast a spell on whoever steps over it. In Africa the fetish is frequently constructed in the form of a man or animal. Among the American Indians it is usually the medicine bundle, a sacred bundle containing an assortment of objects collected by a youth under supernatural guidance.

Few people of today wear fetishes of this nature, but the popularity of the amulet has never faded. Objects favored by primitive peoples are still being worn. Equally popular are talis-

mans, objects whose purpose is to bring good luck rather than
to prevent harm coming to its owner. The four-leaf clover, the
horseshoe, and the rabbit's foot are familiar examples of talismans
in the United States.

Shamans were also called upon for bonesetting and even a
little surgery. Skulls found in late Stone Age sites throughout
America and Europe show that *trephining* operations were performed—that is, holes were cut through the skull with flint or
obsidian instruments to remove pieces of bone. It is clear that
patients survived the ordeal because the rounded edges of the
bone show that the tissues healed after the operation.

Operations similar to trephining are performed by primitive
peoples today to treat chronic migraine and even brain tumors.

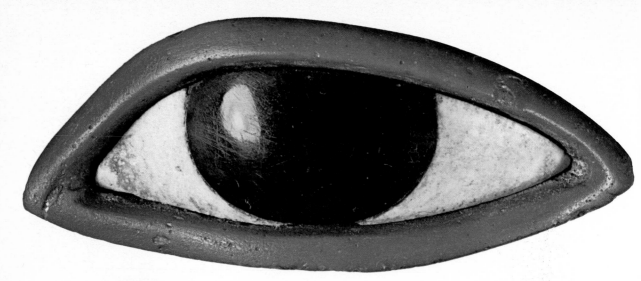

Above: a wood amulet, worn at
all times, from Borneo. When
the owner was ill or distressed,
the local medicine man would
take chips from the amulet and
use them to brew a remedy.

Primitive peoples today also make use of trephining "to let the
demons out." The same reasoning may lie behind some of the
prehistoric operations, for in some of the Stone Age skulls the
position of the holes suggests the same surgical intentions. It may
be that the Chinese art of acupuncture originated many thousands
of years ago for the same purpose—a ritual pricking of the body
"to let the demons out."

The medicine man's healing procedures were magical cere-
monies accompanied by spells and chants. Very often the magic
worked and the sick person recovered. Magic frequently works
for people who expect it to work, and since most people who are
otherwise in good health usually recover from sickness, the
medicine man's reputation as a healer was continually reinforced.
Almost the greatest aid to recovery is the faith that someone
whose power you trust is working on your behalf. This applies
whether the aid is thought to come from God, a spiritual leader,
a trusted doctor or a shaman. It also explains the importance of
a bedside manner to impress the patient and inspire confidence,
whether this be the 20th-century family doctor persuading a
patient his medicine will make him well, or the medicine man
in a forest clearing stamping and shouting through a fearsome
mask.

If a person is suffering from such diseases as beri-beri, scurvy,
or pellagra because of a diet deficiency, faith may be able to
relieve the symptoms for a few days, but faith unaided will not
make up the deficiency. For afflictions of this kind magic on its
own is not enough, and the shaman's knowledge of herbal and
mineral remedies played an essential role.

As superstition hardened into the early pre-Christian religions,
the knowledge of the medicine man became the sacred lore of
the hereditary priesthood. In the fertile valleys of Mesopotamia
and along the Nile, where huge cities, palaces, and temples
towered above the land, the priesthood provided a continuity
of knowledge. Beliefs about disease and its remedies were handed
down from generation to generation, and new ideas were added
to a steadily increasing store. The famous library of the Assyrian
king Ashurbanipal, who lived in the 7th century B.C., contained
over 800 clay tablets concerned with and instructing in the

Left: a favorite Egyptian amulet, meant to stare evil spirits into submission, was the eye—this one taken from a mummy case.

Right: a Sicilian fisherman paints an eye on his boat to ward off evil spirits and bring him safely back to port again.

treatment of illness. They tell much about ancient beliefs.

In Babylon the preliminary examination of a patient was to decide whether his complaint was caused naturally or supernaturally. Wounds, fractures, sores, and other external maladies were considered to be natural in origin and were treated by a nonpriestly healer skilled in herbal and mineral remedies. But if the disease was thought to be the work of one of the numerous demons of Babylonian mythology, the priest-physician would be called in to exercise his sacred art. First he would examine the patient, and then he would consult the omens to help foretell the patient's future. He might look at the conjunction of the stars, or interpret the flickering of a flame or the movement of a drop of oil in water. One of the most celebrated methods was to read the liver of a sheep. It was believed that if a patient breathed into the nostrils of a sheep his or her symptoms would be magically transferred to the sheep's liver. The sheep would then be killed, and the liver removed and examined for any irregularity in shape, color, size, or texture. It was supposed also to register the nature of the illness and show what the patient's chances of recovery were. The priest's findings were recorded by sticking wooden pegs into a clay model of the organ. Some of these models have been excavated, and though they are over 3000 years old, they are considerably more accurate renderings of sheep's livers than the peculiar shapes that passed for human livers in anatomical charts of only 500 years ago.

The Babylonians thought that certain demons were responsible for certain diseases, and special masks and daggers were made to scare them away. The Southwest Wind, personified by an eagle with a dog's body and a lion's paws, was thought to bring a consuming fever. Because he was supposed to be afraid of his own image, clay and metal likenesses of this evil spirit were fixed to doors and windows to ward him off, and protect those inside the house.

Before he could cure a sick person the priest had to attract the attention of the demon responsible by naming him, if possible, and relating his deeds. Uncertainty as to which particular demon was involved sometimes led to the recitation of immense lists of names in the hope that the right one might be included. Having

Above: a carved wooden Central African talisman designed to protect the bearer against the torments of headache, apparently as much a plague of African villages as of modern big cities.

Right: a Babylonian clay model of a sheep's liver used in diagnosis of disease. Readings from the liver, removed from a sheep after a sick person had breathed into its nostrils, were pegged into the model to help with the forecasting of the course of the illness.

Below: Assyrian priestly figure with the knotted whip often used to scare off demons of disease. Priests of Assyria and Babylonia were physicians as well. They believed that disease was an abnormality caused by unseen, external demons, and if members of a family showed similar symptoms, there was obviously a specific demon to blame for it.

obtained the demon's attention, the priest tried to make it leave the sick person by releasing a raven. As the bird soared up to the sky the demon was invited to follow it. Alternatively the demon might be offered a sacrifice as compensation for leaving its human victim. Sometimes a wax image of the patient would be made, and the demon commanded or enticed into entering it. Then the figure containing the demon was taken away to be thrown into the river or burned in a fire.

Sometimes a sound herbal treatment was not considered effective enough, and a medicine with a revolting ingredient would be added to disgust the demon and send it off. One example is the cure prescribed for a complaint that much troubled the Babylonians—soreness of the eyes. This was brought about by the hot wind blowing out of the Arabian desert. The cure was a drink consisting of cut-up onion and beer. This is a sensible enough remedy because onions encourage the flow of cleansing tears. The eyes were also dabbed, again very sensibly, with oil. While this treatment would have been satisfactory in itself, it was not thought to be disgusting enough to repel the Demon of the Southwest Wind. So this ritualistic prescription was added:

"Disembowel a yellow frog, mix its gall with curd, and apply to the eye."

The Ancient Egyptians too considered disease the work of evil spirits. Sometimes it was thought that the soul of a dead person had managed to enter a living body, drinking its blood, gnawing its bones, and consuming its flesh. It was the task of the priest-physician to drive the invading soul away.

Incantations and pleas to the gods can be found on the same papyrus scrolls that list case histories and careful recipes for remedies. Some of these are still in active use today, for example opium, castor oil, and syrup of figs against constipation. (The well-to-do Egyptian of antiquity was a hearty eater and suffered greatly from this disorder.) Other ingredients such as asses' dung and flyspecks have fortunately gone out of fashion. The recipe

Left: a Babylonian bronze statue of about 1000 B.C. of the demon Pazuzu. His hot breath, like the scorching desert wind, brought racking fever to men and animals.

for one of the many cures for baldness sounds more like the witches brew in Shakespeare's *Macbeth*. It includes shell of tortoise, backbone of raven, womb of a she-cat, tadpole from a pool, fat of a black snake, and burnt quills of a hedgehog. Another unappetizing remedy consisted of equal parts of writing ink and fluid from the brain.

But as dynasty followed dynasty on the banks of the Nile the incantations became more elaborate, and the medicinal compounds more and more complicated. This always happens when the art of healing moves too far away from its simple origins. If a healer or apothecary mixes together dozens of different substances his expertise may impress the patient, but it is a sign that the ingredients that work best have probably been forgotten.

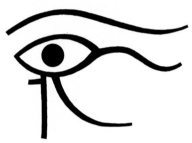

Left: the Eye of Horus, the bird-headed Egyptian god. Seth, the demon of evil, snatched out Horus' eye, but through the intervention of his mother, the sage Thoth restored the eye and its powers. It became the symbol of godly protection and healing.

Above: the symbol for the Eye of Horus was adopted by many Roman physicians to add mystic authority to their work. Gradually the drawing became simplified to the sign ℞, which doctors use to this day at the beginning of their prescriptions.

This is one of the disadvantages of healing with magic. The supernatural treatment by ritual and the natural treatment with physical remedies begin by being inseparable. The physical remedies are believed to act only because of the ritual that accompanies them. But as time passes the magical aspect begins to dominate. The rites are considered sufficient in themselves, and the natural remedies are neglected. Faced with a decline in cures the priest increases the number of essential stages in the magic ritual. If the cure does not work he can blame the patient for the failure on the grounds that the sufferer must have left out some essential phrase or gesture.

Not to be outdone, the apothecary increases the number of ingredients in the remedies and makes them more outlandish. The difficulty of obtaining rare ingredients will explain why remedies that work are hard to get.

In one aspect of modern medicine Egyptian magic continues to be practiced to the present day. When the 20th-century doctor writes out a prescription he prefaces it with the sign ℞. He may think this is an abbreviation of the Latin word *recipe*, but he will be wrong. It is a simplified form of the Egyptian hieroglyph for the Eye of Horus—a symbol familiar as a jewel among the treasures of Tutankamun.

This symbol derives its power from the myth of death and resurrection of the god Osiris. The myth says that after Osiris had been treacherously murdered, his son Horus set out to avenge his death. In the course of the long struggle one of his eyes was plucked out. This was eventually restored by Thoth, the god of wisdom, and came to be linked with the art of healing. Roman physicians introduced Egyptian symbols into their prescriptions to impress their patients, and the eye of Horus was one. It was originally done as shown in the drawing on this page.

Over the centuries the outline was modified until it became the simpler symbol we know today. Unwittingly, then, even the most orthodox of today's doctors make use of a magic sign.

It was the Ancient Greeks who took healing away from the dependence on the supernatural, although the earliest Greek theories were similar to those of other early civilizations. Before medicine and religion were disengaged, the Greeks too believed that disease was caused by the actions of supernatural beings, in this case the god Apollo. The god of healing was his son Aesculapius, who as a youth learned the art from the centaurs. Temples to Aesculapius were built in some of the most picturesque parts of Greece, often near mineral springs. The temples in Cos and Epidaurus were the most famous. The sick were received by priests trained in the arts of healing. Patients were given purifying baths and massage, and then passed a night in the sanctuary of the temple. Here, it was said, the god visited them in a dream, or else his sacred snakes came and licked their wounds. The healing power of nature must have had something to do with any cure, but the most effective part of the treatment was thought to be the visitation of the god.

The 5th century B.C. was the Golden Age of Greece, a time of accomplishment and innovation in many fields of knowledge. Healing was no exception. Hippocrates, born to a priestly family

Below: Aesculapius, the god of healing. In 8th-century Greece he was only a mortal, although a gifted physician. Later he became a god, the son of Apollo. He learned his healing arts from the centaur Cheiron so well that at last Zeus struck him with a thunderbolt, lest he deprive the gods of their power over the life and death of men.

Above: a votive relief dedicated to Aesculapius. Since there is a prominent vein on the leg being offered, possibly the trouble was varicose veins. Such an offering was made either as a petition for healing, or as thanks for having been cured.

Above: a late Roman mosaic of Jesus healing the blind man of Jericho. The ministry of Christ as reported in the Gospels of the New Testament was full of this kind of miracle healing.

on the island of Cos, was a contemporary of Socrates and the Parthenon sculptors. In his treatise *On the Sacred Disease*, which was epilepsy, he wrote that people who believe the gods cause "fevers and delirium and jumpings out of bed . . . make the divinity to be most wicked and impious." He was responsible for introducing simpler remedies into medicine, and his recommendations included plain food, fresh air, and a calm life. He is known as the Father of Medicine, but he has a right to be called the Father of Nature therapy too. Under his influence the temples of Aesculapius became more like modern sanitariums, and the emphasis on the supernatural diminished. "Prayer indeed is good," wrote one of his followers, "but while calling on the gods man should himself lend a hand."

Although the whims of a god were no longer thought responsible for disease, the actual causes were still largely unknown. Many contradictory theories came and went. Some believed that the symptoms associated with a disease were caused by that disease, others that they were brought about by the body's efforts to combat the disease. This meant that supporters of one theory would treat a fever with something to bring it down, while supporters of the rival theory would give something to help the body keep it high. This difference in approach continues today in the two schools of *allopathy* and *homeopathy*. Allopathy is the method of treating disease by medicines that fight the symptoms. It is the method of orthodox medicine. Homeopathy fights disease by treating like with like.

The Jews of the Old Testament were like the early Greeks in believing that disease had a divine origin. But because they worshiped a single God they could not make one divinity responsible for disease and another for curing it. Therefore, they believed that since God was infinitely good and just, the purpose of disease must be to punish sin. A person's illness became a public indication that he was a sinner. This helps us to appreciate the effect of these words to the sick by Jesus, who followed the Jewish precepts:

"Go thy way, thy sins are forgiven thee."

People may no longer believe that God punishes sin by making someone sick, but it is certainly true that people frequently punish themselves by bringing on illness. The work of Freud and the subsequent recognition of psychosomatic disorders show how common it is for men and women to make themselves sick as a punishment for acts or thoughts they are ashamed of. The doctor and analyst Georg Groddeck, who was born in Germany in 1866, used to ask patients who came to him with a broken arm, "Why did you break your arm?" and those with laryngitis, "Why did you wish to be unable to speak?"

Jesus' regard for the sufferings of the poor led to the foundation throughout Christendom of hospitals in which the sick and poverty-stricken could find refuge, even though the treatment they received might be rudimentary. Jesus' sufferings on the cross, however, may have led to a contradictory attitude among some Christians who tended to exalt suffering in the belief that it brought people closer to Jesus. This point of view held that if the sick could bear their pain with good grace

Left: Job with his comforters. Within Christianity the concern for the sick and distressed, shown in Jesus' life, developed along with the contradiction that patient suffering is a virtue. This is clear in the story of Job, who endured all the calamities visited upon him and maintained his faith—for which he was eventually richly rewarded.

Right: St. Lucy, who became the patron saint of eyes. According to one legend, when denounced to the authorities as a Christian by her fiancé, she tore out her own eyes and sent them to him on a plate. But the Virgin Mary miraculously restored her eyes even more beautiful than before.

QVELE POL-
ASTRE SONO
DI S. ANTONIO

MIRACOLO DI S. ANTONIO FVORA DI BRESIA

Left: an 18th-century Italian woodcut of Saint Anthony, the founder of monasticism. As a healer he was associated with the cure of erysipelas, an inflammation that results in bright redness of the face and skin. Though his intercession was said to cure sufferers—especially during the epidemic of 1089—his name has been given to the disease itself, and it is commonly known as "Saint Anthony's fire."

and unwavering faith in God rather than seek relief and cure, their chances of salvation were higher.

The development of Christianity also brought about a revival of a belief in demons. Saint Augustine stated flatly, "All diseases of Christians are to be ascribed to demons; chiefly do they torment the fresh baptized, yea, even the guiltless newborn infant." The devout prayed to the saints to intercede with God to cure their ailments, and certain saints became associated with particular afflictions: Saint Lucy with diseases of the eye, Saint Apollonia with teeth, and so on. Paintings of Saint Agnes, who was supposed to help cure diseases of the breast, show her bearing her two breasts on a dish.

As European civilization sank into the long torpor of the Dark Ages, the most fortunate among the sick were those who lived in the vicinity of monasteries. For, despite repeated condemnations by Popes, monks cultivated herbs and endeavored to practice the simpler forms of healing.

For a thousand years, from the fall of the Roman Empire in A.D. 476 to the dawn of the Renaissance in the 14th century, life in the stinking overcrowded cities and the wild desolate countryside became more dismal than at any time since the end of the Stone Age. It was more fearful too, for this was the period of great epidemics. Leprosy, St. Anthony's fire, St. Vitus dance, influenza, typhus, the sweating sickness—all ravaged the land. Most terrible of all was the plague, which in the form known as the Black Death killed one-third of the population. There was no safe conduct through a calamity of this magnitude. One of the popular if ineffective protections against the plague was the sprinkling of perfumed water on clothes to keep the air around a person pure. Eau de Cologne is a survival of one of these plague waters.

When threatened by a danger against which nothing seemingly can be done and chance is the only hope, belief that an amulet or talisman affords magical protection at least does no harm. During the terrible epidemics, medieval Europeans wore necklaces with special coins, images of the saints, jewels, and fragments of scripture or magic words. The most famous of the magic words is *abracadabra*, a word charm that is known to have existed at least as far back as the 3rd century A.D. Its origin is thought to be the old Hebrew phrase *abrak-ha-dabra*, meaning "I bless the deed." One form of creating a charm out of this word was to make it into a triangle, losing a letter with each line and ending with the single letter "A," as follows:

```
A B R A C A D A B R A
 A B R A C A D A B R
  A B R A C A D A B
   A B R A C A D A
    A B R A C A D
     A B R A C A
      A B R A C
       A B R A
        A B R
         A B
          A
```

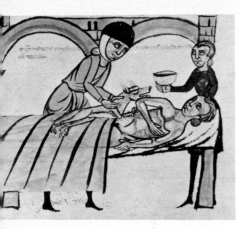

Above: medieval practitioners of medicine who taught at the school of medicine in Salerno, Italy, treated a prolapsed intestine by placing the body of a dying animal on the body of the patient as a kind of poultice. The animal's body provided the needed warmth.

The idea was that with each line the illness would lose hold a little more until finally it would be squeezed out.

A charm like this may only have worked on illnesses that respond to the power of suggestion, but it was certainly more straightforward and less gruesome than some of the treatments prescribed by doctors in the Middle Ages. For example, the following is a cure for gout recommended by Gilbertus Anglicus, an English practitioner:

"Take a very fat puppy and skin him. Then take the juice of wild cucumber, rue, pellitory, ivy berries, juniper berries, spurge, castoreum [grease from a beaver], fat of vulture, goose, fox and bear, in equal parts, and stuff the puppy therewith. Then boil him. Add wax to the grease which floats to the top and apply as an ointment. Or, if you prefer, take a frog when neither sun nor moon is shining, cut off its hind legs and wrap them in deerskin. Apply the frog's right leg to the right foot and the left leg to the left foot of the gouty patient and for certain he will be cured." We might wonder how the one who mixed the brew felt.

Treatments became further complicated by the application of astrology to healing. The cure—and the malady—was said to be influenced by favorable stars and planets. Operations had to be

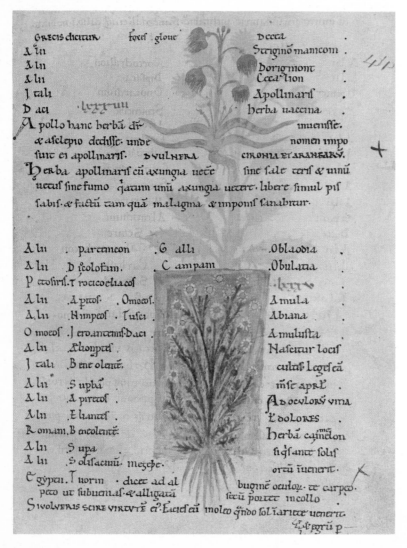

Left: a page from a 12th-century herbal shows plants and their uses. These herbals were meant as a directory of drugs for the use of the physicians, but all the drugs were either plants or plant preparations. These herbals represented centuries of nature lore and experience. The Bodleian Library, Oxford (MS Bodley 130, No. 84).

set for particular times of the astrological year. Plants had to be gathered in particular months and at night. This last practice originated in the belief that the plant should not observe the person coming to pick it. To lull the plant's suspicions even further it was sometimes thought best to approach the plant backward. The English book that developed these astrological theories to their highest point was Nicholas Culpeper's *Herbal*. It became so famous that it is still in print, and it has enjoyed a longer success than any other prose work except the King James Bible.

According to Culpeper, whose book was published in the mid-17th century, each disease is caused by a planet, and can therefore be cured by a herb belonging to an opposing planet. For example:

"Mushrooms are under the dominion of Saturn and if any are poisoned by eating them, Wormwood as an herb of Mars cures him, because Mars is exalted in Capricorn, the House of Saturn." (It should be added that this cure is not likely to work.)

Adding another complication to the choice of treatment was the popular Doctrine of Signatures. According to this theory, certain plants give an indication of their use by color, shape, or other markings. Nature or God has made a kind of visual pun to let us know that, for example, plants with a yellow sap serve as a cure for jaundice, those with spotted leaves cure the bites of spotted snakes, and plants bearing heart-shaped leaves, like the trefoil, benefit the heart. As late as 1657 the English botanist William Cole could write:

"*Wall-nuts* have the perfect Signature of the Head: The outer husk or green Covering, represent the *Pericranium*, or outward skin of the skull, whereon the hair groweth, and therefore salt made of those husks or barks, are exceeding good for wounds in the head . . . The *Kernel* hath the very figure of the Brain, and therefore it is very profitable for the Brain, and resists poysons; for if the Kernel be bruised, and moystned with the quintessence of Wine, and laid upon the Crown of the Head, it comforts the brain and head mightily."

The belief that plants have even been distributed for our convenience still survives, especially in the idea that dock plant leaves always grow near stinging nettles to be handy for treating stings. Anyone who has had to cover the ground in the vicinity of nettles in an anxious and unrewarding search for dock plants will know how unreliable this idea is. Incidentally, though cooling to the skin, dock leaves have no effect on the sting. The juice from a honeysuckle leaf is actually much more effective in relieving the pain.

The 18th century discarded the more extravagant claims of magical curing just as it curtailed the fantastic excesses of the drug makers. Even so, such items as powdered crabs' eyes, with which King William III of England dusted his boils, wood lice, pearls, ground coral, lion's fat, and virgin's milk were among the last to go. Orthodox medicine was able to advance once it became possible to study anatomy, and with the development of aseptic surgery, anesthetics, and sterilization, orthodox medicine started on its long series of triumphs.

Disease was attributed to a material cause at this period, and

Below: gathering herbs to make medicines. The process of picking the plants became complicated as the mystique associated with their medical use grew and was elaborated. Herbs had to be picked at the appropriate time— often only in the moonlight so that the earth would be less aware of the plants being taken.

ALTISSIMVS
CREAVIT DE TERRA MEDECINAMET VIR
PRVDENS NON ABHOREBIT ILLAM
ANNO DOMMINI 1623

Above: the painted signboard of a surgeon-physician of 17th-century
England with his specialties—urinalysis, amputation, dentistry,
etc.—displayed in the illustrations around the portrait of the
medical man himself. By this time, medicine was turning its back
on its magical mystique, and becoming a rigorously defined science.

could therefore be treated by material means. Exceptions to this attitude were pushed aside as outside the province of doctors. Miracle cures and faith healing were dismissed as survivals of superstition practiced by quacks on a gullible public. It required the striking increase in stress diseases and psychosomatic disorders for the influence of the nonmaterial mind on the material body to become the object of sustained research.

From being condemned as a charlatan, the medicine man became the ancestor of all healers. Experiments were even conducted on the success of magic versus medicine to cure warts. Warts are caused by a viral infection, but are well known for their response to the power of suggestion. Countless cures for them can be found in the folklore of all countries. Such cures usually involve touching or rubbing the warts with a piece of meat, a snail, a frog, a potato, a bean, or some other perishable item. The item is then buried in the ground, and the warts disappear as it decays.

This remedy transfers the warts to some other object. Other kinds of remedies transfer the warts to another person. Henry E. Sigerist, historian of medicine and one of the earliest to comment favorably on the achievements of magic, tells of a cure for warts that was told to him. "Buy a new silk ribbon. Make as many knots as the child has warts. Drop the ribbon in the vicinity of a school where many children pass by. A girl will pick up the ribbon and with it your daughter's warts."

Sigerist remarks that although this advice was not very charitable, it was effective. He goes on to point out that this cure is a good example of the survival of primitive procedures in 20th-century folk medicine. No incantations are made, but otherwise the ritual would be recognized by a priest of Babylon, a primitive Saxon, or an American Indian. The ribbon must be new and of silk. In other words it must cost money, and is a sacrifice. The disease is fastened in the ribbon through the magic knots. Finally a transplanting takes place from one individual to another by means of the magical token.

Professor H. J. Eysenck of London's Maudsley Hospital conducted an experiment to compare magic with orthodox treatment. The magic employed was basically similar to the old abracadabra ritual.

"Two groups of children were used: the control group which received ordinary treatment for their warts; and the experimental group which was submitted to suggestion treatment. This consisted essentially in drawing a picture of the child's hand, with the wart on it, on a large sheet of paper; and then, with a certain amount of hocus-pocus, drawing circles around the wart and reducing its size on the picture day by day until the wart had completely disappeared in the picture. This procedure, which makes use of suggestibility no less than the famous method used by Tom Sawyer in *Huckleberry Finn*, was shown to be far more effective than the orthodox medical treatment."

Why suggestion treatment and hocus-pocus should work in the case of warts is unknown. The fact that an affliction with a material cause, a virus, can be cured by nonmaterial means should, however, encourage healers to consider how else the magic of the past can still be used.

Above: in rejecting the so-called primitive beliefs, modern medicine rejected many traditional remedies like the one that a live snail placed on a wart will make it go away. Some old cures, against all scientific rationale, seem to work amazingly frequently.

Nature as Healer

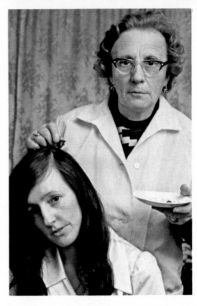

Many people today believe that the remedies of nature are the safest and most suitable for man—who is himself a part of Nature. Animals instinctively seek out the means to cure themselves. Dr. D. C. Jarvis comments on this in the opening chapter of *Folk Medicine*, his celebrated book on the virtues of a diet of honey and cider vinegar, published in 1958. He said: "I have come to marvel at the instinct of animals to make use of natural laws for healing themselves. They know unerringly which herbs will cure what ills. Wild creatures first seek solitude and absolute relaxation, then they rely on the complete remedies of Nature—the medicine in plants

For healers who rely upon the world of nature for their cures, the types of "medicines" can be unnervingly wide, ranging from hot baths to bee stings by bees especially bred for the purpose. Above: Mrs. Julia Owen, an Austrian-born healer, learned bee therapy from her medical family. She is shown placing a bee on the head of a woman registered as blind. Mrs. Owen has an impressive list of patients whose sight has been greatly improved after their treatment by bee stings. Right: a healing bee sets to work.

compelling her babies in a rainy spell to eat leaves of the spice bush; an animal, bitten by a poisonous snake, confidently chewing snakeroot—all these are typical examples. An animal with fever quickly hunts up an airy, shady place near water, there remaining quiet, eating nothing but drinking often until its health is recovered. On the other hand, an animal bedevilled by rheumatism finds a spot of hot sunlight and lies in it until the misery bakes out."

The ability of animals to select what they need can be uncanny. Lord Ritchie-Calder records in his book *Medicine and Man* that "sheep with a diet deficient in lime have been known to eat, with geometrical exactitude, the grass of a squared plot which had been limed, before turning to other pastures which would satisfy their hunger but lacked the subtler medical requirements. On the South African veldt, cattle were dying of a mysterious epidemic. One group survived and it was found that they were eating the bark and herbage of a tree in the trunk of which there was a single copper nail. The rest of the cattle were sick from a deficiency of minute traces of copper."

It is not known how humans lost this instinctive ability to recognize what they need to keep healthy. The loss is usually associated with the development of the cerebral cortex, the area of the brain that enables us to reason. The growth of this part of the brain is what accounts for the difference in appearance between the low sloping forehead of Neanderthal Man and the high vertical forehead of present-day peoples. Reason enables us to plan our behavior, choosing from alternative courses of action the one that seems most beneficial to us in the long term. But this sometimes brings reason into conflict with instincts. When escaping from a predator, instinct might urge us to run up the valley, while reason tells us to dodge behind a nearby rock and double back. Successes brought about by the use of reason led to a decline in the reliance on instinct. Distinguishing between safe and unsafe foods, for example, became a matter of teaching and learning from generation to generation.

In recent years mankind's development has come to be seen as a mixed blessing. A wide range of diseases have come out of medical treatment intended to cure other diseases. These are known as *iatrogenic* ailments, the word being taken from the Greek *iatros*, a physician. One such disease arises from lengthy treatment with the drug cortisone, hailed as the wonder cure for arthritis. This drug puffs out the face, brings skin rashes and ulcers, and reduces the body's resistance to infection. Many viruses have developed strains that are resistant to the drugs used in their treatment, and these require larger dosages or different drugs to combat them. There are certain antibiotics that have been found to damage the liver or cause anemia, and some treatments for anemia that cause tumors. The most infamous drug of all is thalidomide, the so-called safe sleeping pill that was responsible in recent years for the birth of hundreds of deformed babies. The list goes on, and doubt has even been thrown on the safety of the widely used penicillin.

Such dangers of modern drugs may encourage us to look at the arguments of those who believe that all treatment for illness

Above: Hippocrates, who believed that disease and cure were both natural processes, with Galen, the last of the ancient physicians.

Above: this Ancient Greek bas-relief depicts a sick person being cured in a temple of Aesculapius, where patients stayed overnight. It was believed that healing resulted from a visit of the god in a dream, or from being licked by the god's sacred snakes during sleep. Right: Aesculapius discovers betony, a medicinal plant, as depicted in a 9th-century manuscript. By this time natural remedies were being used.

should be as natural as possible. Among these are the naturo-paths. They believe that we should lead a simple life free from stress and worry, and get plenty of fresh air and exercise. Diet should be confined to the natural foods the body needs, un-contaminated by artificial fertilizers and chemical additives. They maintain that in this way we will build up a strong sound constitution that will not easily succumb to illness. If illness should occur, however, the body, being basically fit, will be able to recover by natural means without drugs or operations.

Many of the ideas on which naturopathy is based go back a long way. About 2500 years ago the Greek physician Hippo-crates declared his belief in the life force, a healing power within the body that worked to restore the balance of health. Certain things encouraged the life force. Other things, such as overeating, discouraged it. To encourage it, Hippocrates and his followers recommended fresh air, a plain diet with only occasional use of spices to "purge the head and lungs" by sneezing, massage, water treatment, and wine or barley water as drinks. These recommendations would all find favor with today's naturopaths, except perhaps for the wine.

Water is the most natural cure of all. People have recognized its value from prehistoric times, and have made use of it to soothe their various aches and wounds. Long before Hippo-crates lived, the Ancient Greeks built sanctuaries dedicated to Aesculapius, the god of medicine, to which the sick came for help. Although there were various rites associated with the god, the patient was treated at a practical level in a way that re-sembles a modern nature cure. He was given a careful diet, plenty of fresh air and relaxation in peaceful surroundings, and a program of massage and bathing. Frequently the temple was near a mineral or hot spring, and there the patient might also drink the water as part of his cure.

The Romans took over the idea of bathing from the Greeks, and the Roman emperors built vast public baths or *thermae* which were available to all Romans for a small charge. Social life revolved around these palatial buildings where ordinary men and women could enjoy the hot baths, cold baths, vapor and shower baths. There was no soap, but slaves scraped the backs of the rich with special instruments called strigils. The poor had to do their own back rubbing against the walls. Attached to the baths were gymnasiums, parks, libraries, and restaurants.

The early Christians held that hot baths led to wickedness, and the thermae fell into ruins. Christians raised no objection to cold water, however. Pagan Europe had many healing wells or springs, dedicated to various local deities, and these were often rededicated by missionaries to Christian saints. Pilgrims drank the water or dipped their body in it. Crutches were sometimes left hanging on a nearby tree as a sign of a cure.

By the 14th century doctors had again begun to interest them-selves in the waters of the old Roman baths. Throughout the centuries, of course, peasants had made use of them to cure bowel disorders and rheumatism, and to dissolve stones in the bladder. Some waters were especially renowned for removing the curse of barrenness in women. In England the Roman baths

Above: the *Fountain of Youth*, a painting by the 16-century German Lucas Cranach, shows how old women become young girls after a dip in the magical waters. Belief in a fountain of youth was once worldwide, and many dreamed of finding the longed-for waters that could restore youth to them.

Right: a 19th-century view of taking the waters in Bath, England. The Roman baths that fell into decay were dug out of the swamps and received a new lease of life after the Dark Ages when the gentry and nobility began to visit Bath in hopes of being cured of a variety of ailments, real and imagined. Soon it became a social attraction as well as a place for healing, where, as one dour reporter in the 18th century remarked, "is performed all the wanton dalliances imaginable."

Above: Vincenz Preissnitz, the Water Demon of Gräfenberg. His cold water cures were rigorous and demanding. Patients were housed in stark and comfortless lodgings, and treatment included being wrapped in cold wet sheets; the falling douche, in which cold water was dumped on the sufferer from a height of 11–19 feet; and a variety of baths: sitz baths, plunge baths, and the ascending douche—a kind of icy cold bidet.

in the city of Bath were gradually resurrected out of the swamp that had engulfed them. In Germany and Switzerland, many places containing baths began to draw patrons of both sexes. At Baden-in-Argau in the 15th century men and women bathed almost nude and cavorted in the water with joyful abandon. No doubt this freedom played a part in the cure for barrenness.

By 1580 the French scholar Montaigne was able to set off on a lengthy tour of the spas of Europe in the hope of finding a water to dissolve his kidney stone. He found hot springs and warm springs, and waters that tasted of liquorice or iron, alum or sulphur. Almost everywhere he noted the excessively high fees charged to visitors.

By the later 16th century doctors had come to believe in the medicinal properties of the waters from many mineral springs, and encouraged their patients to drink them. The cult of the water cure spread. Throughout Europe, and later New England, mineral springs were discovered or rediscovered, enclosed within a bath house, and advertised. If the water found public favor the local community prospered, and many towns owe their origin to a mineral spring. Even when the waters themselves had little curative powers, the chances of recovering health at a spa were often higher than could be expected from the remedies of a doctor of that time. The change of air, the check on overeating, and the interest of the journey might all play a part in improving the condition of a patient.

It was the 19th century that saw systemization of the modern water cure by Vincenz Preissnitz. It was based on the wetting and sweating therapies that had been practiced by peasants for hundreds of years. Preissnitz was born in 1799, the son of a farmer in the small Austrian town of Gräfenberg—now part of Czechoslovakia and called Jesenik. At the age of 18 his ribs were crushed by a wagon, and doctors declared his case hopeless. Preissnitz cured himself by keeping a cold wet compress to his chest for a year. He then began to apply this principle of cold water to other afflictions, and was soon curing so many people that the local peasants suspected him of practicing magic. They placed broomsticks across his doorway to see whether, like a true sorcerer, he could leave his house without dislodging them. The local doctors were furiously opposed to his work, and repeatedly brought him to court on charges of unlawful practice. On one occasion a miller, speaking on his behalf, said: "They have all helped me, the doctors, the apothecaries, and Preissnitz. The doctors and apothecaries helped me to get rid of my money and Preissnitz to get rid of my illness."

Preissnitz believed that disease was caused by the existence of morbid matter in the blood. The aim of his treatment was to help nature get rid of poisonous substances without hindrance from medicine. This could be done by provoking a series of crises such as sweating, vomiting, diarrhea, or skin eruptions to rid the body of impurities. The waters in Gräfenberg, where Preissnitz lived, contained no distinctive minerals. They were used simply as water. Cold water, particularly when applied in the form of cold wet sheets wrapped around the body, at first drives the blood away from the surface. Gradually the blood returns to the surface and begins to warm up the wet

sheets. It was believed that this promoted a better circulation and encouraged the sweat flow that can help to rid the body of infection.

Preissnitz introduced new varieties of water treatment such as the sitz bath, the plunge bath and, apparently most successful in producing crisis, the falling douche. In this treatment a thick column of cold water hurtled down on the patient's back from a considerable height. One patient likened this experience to standing under a "falling load of gravel."

The regime at Gräfenberg was harsh. The water treatment was supplemented by exposure to mountain air and plenty of exercise. Living conditions were extremely rough and there were no amenities. Despite this, Preissnitz' fame was enormous. According to the English author E. S. Turner, whose entertaining book *Taking the Cure* was published in 1967, Preissnitz' patients in one year included "One royal highness, one duke, one duchess, 22 princes and princesses, 149 counts and countesses, 88 barons and baronesses, 14 generals, 53 staff officers, 196 captains and subalterns, 104 high and low civil servants, 65 divines, 46 artists, and 87 physicians and apothecaries."

Water cures, such as those practiced by Preissnitz, held no hope of success for lung patients. They placed their faith in finding a suitable climate—though what constituted a suitable climate was a matter of some controversy. For a long time wealthy consumptives from England followed the sun, wintering in the South of France, Italy, or Madeira. But in the mid-19th century doctors had discovered that dry frosty air was even better for lung patients, and sufferers flocked to the Alps. Robert Louis Stevenson, the English author of *Treasure Island*, was persuaded to winter in Davos, Switzerland in 1880. He spent a bored and disconsolate six months and wrote of it:

> "Shut in a kind of damned hotel,
> Discountenanced by God and man;
> The food?—Sir, you would do as well
> To cram your belly full of bran."

The mid-19th century also saw the administration of sun-and-air treatment to health seekers by the Swiss healer Arnold Rikli. In his lakeside establishment in Veldes in the Alps, patients passed the night in three-sided huts open to the elements. In the daytime they walked barefoot, and dressed in loose porous clothes to take "air baths," or lay almost naked

Above: a contemporary view of Preissnitz treating health seekers by massaging their limbs with a sponge and cold water. At first Preissnitz ran into considerable opposition from the local medical men, but they were thwarted when the Imperial Home Office sent a commission from Vienna which reported that Preissnitz was to be encouraged to continue his work. Thereafter his colony grew.

Below: one version of the falling douche. For women the falling douche was modified, but for men the force of the water was overwhelming. Sometimes there was a pole for the patient to hang onto, which helped him avoid being knocked flat. This douche was recommended to last from two to ten minutes, but some hardy souls managed to endure it for nearly an hour.

Right: besides the cold water, patients under Preissnitz's regime were expected to take long walks barefoot, unhindered by any kind of heavy clothing.

Left: after the rigors of some forms of health treatment, the advocates of fresh air and sun as the high road to health found willing disciples. Although the sexes were definitely separated, such cures allowed a degree of freedom available almost nowhere else in the 19th century.

in the sun—a most unusual occurrence in the 19th century. The regime at Veldes was strict, and no medicine, alcohol, tea, or coffee was allowed. The whole emphasis was on air breathing. Rikli believed that the air bath invigorated the nervous system, while the sun bath purified the blood.

Adolf Just's method of treatment in his health colony in the Harz mountains in the late 19th century was even more extreme. Patients would exercise without any clothes on, even in heavy rain. In winter they would rub themselves all over with snow. They were encouraged to bathe naked, and to submerge themselves up to their necks in earth for several hours at a time as a life-enhancing process.

The most famous of these 19th century back-to-nature cures, however, was prescribed by Father Sebastian Kneipp, the burly, sharp-eyed parish priest of the Bavarian town of Wöris-hofen. Father Kneipp adapted the principles of Preissnitz by using a watering can to pour cold water onto parts of the body. He also required his patients to walk barefoot every morning through the dewy fields. In the winter they walked barefoot in the snow. By the time he died in 1897 a craze for walking barefoot had spread around the world.

It sometimes takes an effort to realize that these harsh fresh-air-and-water cures were the immediate predecessors of the Health Hydros of today—luxury establishments at luxury prices where overweight businessmen or overwrought movie stars refresh themselves with a carefully meager diet, cold packs, and hot saunas. But this is the expensive end of the market. Naturopaths have also taken up many of these ideas, and naturopathy claims to offer more than a two-week break without food. It is a way of life, and a plan to prevent disease as well as to cure it. Its theories are diametrically opposed to those of orthodox medicine.

Naturopaths speak with admiration of a neglected Frenchman, Professor Antoine Bechamp, who was born in 1816 and lived till 1908. They claim that his work on microbiology in the 1860s was plagiarized by Louis Pasteur, who misunderstood his findings and sent orthodox medicine down the wrong path.

Pasteur provided orthodox medicine with a theory to account for the spread of disease. He isolated certain microorganisms in diseased tissue, notably those of anthrax and rabies, and concluded that these germs had invaded the tissue and caused the

Below: Father Sebastian Kniepp. He recommended that his patients walk barefoot on wet surfaces like wet grass, wet stones, and fresh snow. He prescribed three minutes in snow as a cure for chilblains.

disease. Bechamp, however, maintained that these organisms were not germs but "scavengers" that had "invaded the body in an effort to rid it of the accumulated waste products and other morbid matters which were producing a lowered vitality." The body produced the illness, and then the scavengers appeared.

Most people nowadays are conditioned to the idea that germs cause disease, and to them the Bechamp theory has every appearance of putting the cart before the horse. But even Pasteur toward the end of his life readily admitted that the state of the human body in which the germ may or may not flourish is as important as the germ in causing a disease. Why are some people able to resist even the most infectious diseases, or suffer only mildly from them, while others readily succumb? The likely explanation seems to be that some people are in a better physical and mental shape to combat the disease.

Naturopaths believe that disease develops because the body has become unable to dispose of its waste products. Toxins or poisons accumulate in the cells, the blood performs its functions inefficiently, and waste products gather in the organs. This leads to fevers, inflammations, and other troubles. Nothing must be given to a patient to curtail the workings of these fevers because they are the body's efforts to cure itself. They represent the healing crisis.

If the healing crisis is treated with drugs, the symptoms will only be suppressed, not cured. The body's efforts to rid itself of the poisons will then have been frustrated, and the long-term consequence will be chronic diseases such as rheumatism and arthritis. On the other hand, certain natural substances may be given to encourage the healing crisis. Cold water baths may be taken for the same purpose. Each healing crisis—and there are likely to be many—eliminate some of the offending toxins. After a series of these crises the toxins and other waste products will have gone, and the body can start the process of regenerating damaged tissue and regaining proper health.

A popular handbook called *Naturopathic Practice* by James Hewlett-Parsons was published in 1968. It makes this significant comment on the curing process:

"Very often a patient suffering from the chronic conditions of which we have written will find in a very short time that he is feeling very much worse than when he first came for treatment. This is where the importance of having the patient's co-operation comes in. The facts must be explained to him and he must be told what to expect in advance and not left to find himself suddenly experiencing distressing symptoms which in his ignorance can frighten him into discontinuing the treatment without further consultation with the practitioner. Correct naturopathic treatment will bring the chronic condition to the surface and the patient must be prepared for this. Acute symptoms may manifest themselves in the shape of fevers, skin eruptions, etc. Headaches and internal turmoil will occur, and all these the patient must bear with fortitude, having been given confidence in advance by his practitioner." In other words, the practitioner must somehow convince his patients that they have the power to cure themselves.

Homeopathy as a healing treatment has much in common

Above: the modern nature cure is most often designed not for the diseased or enfeebled body, but for the fat one. The overweight, the overwrought, and the bored retreat for a week or more into a world of luxurious surroundings, elaborate equipment, and very little food—weak tea and much yogurt seems to be a prominent part of the typical menu. There are Turkish baths, exercise machines, and underwater massage: nature in a most expensive form.

The rigors of the modern health farm, like those of their less polished predecessors, continue to draw patients willing to endure the course of treatment and convinced that they have actually benefited from it. For many hard-pressed executives— and refugees from other tension-provoking walks of life—simply having a week away from all the external pressures is therapy in itself, a kind of monastic retreat for an overstressed body.

Above: a modern homeopathic dispensary. Although some of the homeopathic remedies are poisonous, they are dispensed in minute doses—according to homeopathic thought, the more minute, the more effective.
Below: Samuel Hahnemann, the founder of homeopathy. He was a physician who became disgusted by the inefficiency of orthodox medicine, and on his discovery of how quinine worked, was led to believe that "like cures like."

with naturopathy, although it uses medicines in minute quantities. It was founded by Samuel Hahnemann, who was born in Meissen, Germany in 1755. He was an erudite and religious man, a linguist, a physician, and a chemist. At the age of 35 he happened to try out on himself the powers of quinine. To his surprise he developed symptoms of fever that seemed to him the same as the fever for which quinine was used as a cure. He performed some experiments with other substances, and came to the conclusion that "like cures like."

"It is only by their power to make sick, that drugs can cure sickness: and that a medicine can only cure such morbid conditions as it can produce when tested on healthy persons," he said.

Hahnemann believed that the proper drug acted by setting up an antagonistic fever which fought against the illness. In 1796 he named his new method of treatment homeopathy from two Greek words, *homios* meaning like, and *pathos* meaning *suffering*.

Hahnemann distrusted the massive doses and strange mixtures of drugs meted out to the sick by the doctors of his time. His remedies were single, uncompounded animal, vegetable, or mineral substances. Because they each consisted of one drug only, they were called "simples." He scrupulously tested his drugs on the healthy before using them on the sick. In doing so, he found to his surprise that by decreasing the amount administered, the effectiveness of the drug was not diminished. On the contrary, the smaller the dose, the greater

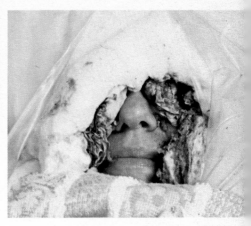

Left: Mrs. Julia Owens, whose bee-stinging remedy seems to help some cases of blindness, also treated British television actor Jack Warner for arthritis. She used the stinging bees on the homeopathic theory that bee stings produce arthritislike swellings. But the bees Mrs. Owens uses are not the ordinary garden bees whose stings can be very dangerous—her bees are especially bred and fed for the particular ailments they treat.

Above: another of Mrs. Owens' remedies is the herbal pack, shown in treating sinus trouble. She also has a herbal pack designed for helping asthmatics.

the effect seemed to be even when the amount was decreased almost to nothing. This finding became known as the Law of Potencies, and it proved to be one of the greatest stumbling blocks in the spread of homeopathic ideas. Many people found it impossible to believe that such tiny amounts, diluted over and over again, could have any effect at all on a patient. Despite this skepticism, however, and despite much personal abuse and hounding, Hahnemann eventually became an internationally respected figure. Homeopathy was well-established in many countries before his death.

The homeopath has several hundred drugs at his disposal, but only about 12 of these are needed for general use. They are all selected on the like cures like principle. For example, the bite of the black spider, a native of Cuba and the states around the Gulf of Mexico, produces an inflamed pimple that becomes an abscess and resembles a carbuncle. Therefore, according to a recent casebook on homeopathic practice, "if you find carbuncles in patients, you may be quite certain that you will be able to disperse them rapidly with a few minute doses of the poison of the black spider or *Tarentula cubensis*."

Similarly, because the effect of a bee sting is to produce symptoms "similar to those of rheumatism, kidney disease, peritonitis, and meningitis," homeopaths believe these conditions can be cured by minute doses of *Apis* or bee virus. In still another case, the poisonous black berries of the deadly nightshade *Atropa belladonna* cause various unpleasant symptoms to develop including a smooth, bright scarlet skin—

Left: diet played an important part for nature healers from the start. They were ahead of their time in recognizing that we are what we eat—though perhaps not quite so visibly as in this fantastic head by a 16th-century painter, Arcimboldi. But our diet is more often chosen by the fashion of the day than by recognition of the needs of the human body. Certainly the traditional diet of our ancestors—vast quantities of starch, and meat if possible, but scarcely any fresh fruit or vegetables—led to perpetual discomfort and indigestion.

Below: *The Cholic*, a caricature by Cruikshank. The starch-laden diet of rich and poor alike brought constipation in its wake. In the 17th century, as Pepys records in his *Diary*, it was common to retire to your chamber for a few days every two or three weeks to take powerful laxatives.

"therefore certain types of scarlet fever . . . are cured by Bella-donna within a day or two."

Hahnemann was unable to explain why the minute doses of his drugs worked. He could only demonstrate, by citing successful cases, that they did. Like the naturopaths, he believed that an important part of a doctor's task was to build up the strength and confidence of his patients, and then to trust in the healing power of the life force. He believed in treating the patient rather than the disease, and tried to find out as much as possible about each patient's temperament, constitution, background, and needs. Present-day homeopathic doctors encourage new patients to talk about their life and their family, their work and their feelings. It may well be that this attentive attitude helps to put patients into a better frame of mind, and start them on the road to curing themselves.

In speculating on why people become ill, Hahnemann came to believe that illness is a way of expressing something by a patient, and that it is the doctor's task not merely to remove the symptoms, but also to find the underlying cause. In this, as Brian Inglis points out in his book *Fringe Medicine*, "he was far in advance of his time, anticipating Freud's discoveries—and even Freud's method of treatment."

Even when the reason for a disease is found and a cure suggested, the treatment can take a long time to gain acceptance. One well known case is that of scurvy. This fatal and painful disease is caused by lack of Vitamin C, a substance that occurs in several vegetables and fruits, particularly in citrus fruit. As long ago as 1593, the English admiral Sir Richard Hawkins, son of the Elizabethan pirate and explorer Sir John Hawkins, said of scurvy: "That which I have seen most fruitful for this sickness is sour oranges and lemons." No attention was paid to this inspired observation, and tens of thousands more sailors died before James Lind, a British naval surgeon, showed that the disease could easily be cured by including mustard cress, tamarinds, oranges, or lemons in the diet. The Admiralty took no notice. That was in 1753. Twenty years later Captain Cook sailed around the world without a case of scurvy among his crew because he followed Lind's advice and carried fresh fruit on board. But not until 30 more years had passed was the drinking of lemon juice made compulsory in the British fleet.

In view of the strong link between scurvy and the limited diet while at sea it is surprising that in 1912 Captain Robert Scott, a British naval captain, failed to take lemon juice or anything else that would prevent scurvy on his journey to the South Pole. He and his men died of exhaustion—but lack of Vitamin C contributed to the exhaustion. Forty years later one of the surviving members of the Expedition, the geologist Sir Raymond Priestley, recalled that ill-fated "dash for the Pole" in these words: "The weather was unkind. Nevertheless scurvy was the decisive factor. Under man-hauling conditions four months is about as long as men hauling sledges can live on rations completely devoid of Vitamin C. Once that period elapsed, nervous and physical deterioration were bound to set in, sores would refuse to heal and lassitude would supervene." This was exactly the fate that overtook Scott and his companions— a fate, moreover, that could have been avoided.

Our knowledge of vitamins is still far from complete, and great claims have been made recently for the curative value of unnaturally high doses of them. A massive intake of Vitamin E is believed to relieve muscular dystrophy. Rheumatism, arthritis, and hepatitis are said to "respond well" to massive doses of Vitamin C. A doctor in North Carolina is reported to give patients crippled by arthritis as much as 10 grams a day, 200 times the accepted average dose. Few other doctors think that the human body can take advantage of such a vast amount at one time.

From the infinitesimally minute potencies of homeopathy

Below: Molière, French playwright and actor in a role as Pourceaugnac the Apothecary. He has a huge purging syringe over his shoulder. With the notion that disease was something which could be flushed out of the body, purges were a popular cure for many suffering from constipation.

to the tremendously heavy doses of vitamin therapy—unorthodox medicine goes to both extremes.

However, if agreement is lacking about what we should take, there is increasing certainty about what we should not. In recent years people have come to recognize the shortcomings of a plastic-packed and chemically preserved diet in which food is artificially flavored, artificially colored, and artificially tenderized. An experiment has been conducted in which a group of chickens was fed on a well-known breakfast cereal. A second group was given the shredded empty packets. The chickens fed on the packets fared better.

A few voices have always been raised in warning against the effect of pesticides and additives in food. Scientists and farmers dismissed such prophets as cranks. Then in 1963 public concern was stirred by Rachel Carson's *Silent Spring*, a book in which she described the horrifying slaughter caused notably by DDT. She pleaded that the destruction of pests be carried out by biological instead of chemical means. Killing the scale insect on the citrus trees of California by means of its natural predator, the lady beetle, is both safer and more efficient than a chemical spray, she explained. "As matters stand now," she wrote, "we are in little better position than the guests of the Borgias." In other words, we are being poisoned.

Since Rachel Carson's death in 1964 another three-letter substance has come to prominence as extremely dangerous. This is PCB, standing for polychlorinated biphenyls. PCB is not a pesticide, but a component of paints and varnish. It also

Left: dosing sailors with lime-juice as a preventive against scurvy on an Arctic expedition. Although an English admiral early suggested citrus fruit as a cure for the condition—a result of a deficiency of vitamin C—it was 50 years before this simple remedy was made official policy.

Right: Dr. Linus Pauling, the Nobel Prize winner. He has also become well-known for his advocacy of massive doses of vitamin C for general well-being and to combat the common cold.

helps to color plastics, and is found in high-temperature lubricating oils. First discovered in the tissues of pike fish in Sweden, PCB has since been located in small but increasing quantities in almost every living thing. The research worker who investigated the PCB frequencies, Sören Jensen, asked the Swedish National Museum of Natural History to give him snippets of the tail feathers of eagles in their collection, together with the date of the bird's death. He found that before 1944 eagles were free of PCB. After 1944 they, and we, have all been contaminated. The alarming feature of this pollution is that PCB has been shown to be five times more potent than DDT in its effect on the sex hormones governing infertility.

There is little one can do about a poison that floats in the air and can be absorbed through the skin. However, it makes good sense to select foods that are best for health, and to avoid or limit intake of those known to be harmful. This is not always easy, both because unhealthy eating habits are often ingrained and because healthier food often costs more.

But let the last word be with the author of *Folk Medicine*. Although in the following quotation Dr. Jarvis is discussing the relative merits of honey and white sugar, his remarks apply equally to every choice between valuable and damaging food. He says: "I am saddened when people tell me they don't eat honey because it cost more than white sugar. I try to make them see that health is not to be had for the asking. Good health is earned. In the long run you must pay either the grocer or the drugstore."

4

The Power of Faith

For Christians, Jesus set the pattern of miracle healing, and down the centuries since his crucifixion his followers have trusted in other men who claim to carry on his healing mission. Right: a Roman ivory diptych showing the miracles of Christ. Among them are pictured the Healing of the Blind, the Man Sick of the Palsy, the Leper, and the Raising of Lazarus.

"And there came a leper to him, beseeching him, and kneeling down to him, and saying unto him, If thou wilt, thou canst make me clean. And Jesus, moved with compassion put forth his hand, and saith unto him, I will; be thou clean. And as soon as he had spoken, immediately the leprosy departed from him, and he was cleansed." *(Mark 1)*.

In the Western world the cures of Jesus are probably the best-known examples of miracle healing. Jesus regarded healing the sick as an integral part of his ministry. The method he favored, we learn from the New Testament, was the laying on of hands. It was a method widely used by healers

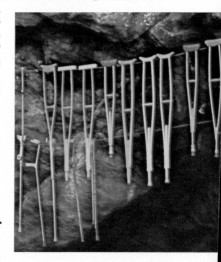

Above: the crutches left behind by those healed at the shrine of Lourdes in France act as a symbol of hope to the power of faith for others who come to the shrine to pray for health.

"Records of healing abound in the early Church"

throughout the ancient world. In curing the blind, however, he practiced a different technique. He spat on the eyes of the blind man at Bethsaida, and in the case of the man born blind, he spat on the ground and anointed the man's eyes with his spittle mixed with clay. The circumstances of the cure also varied. He cured the man with the withered hand in front of a crowd, telling him to "Rise up and stand forth in the midst." But he took the deaf stammerer away from the crowd to a private place to heal him.

Some people were cured because they had faith in Jesus, and sometimes the faith of the sick person's friends was also important. An example of this was when the friends of the man with palsy worked hard to uncover the roof of the house to let the invalid down on a bed before Jesus. In the case of the boy with a dumb spirit, it was his father who prayed, "Lord I believe; help thou my unbelief."

When Jesus charged his disciples to continue his ministry, their duty to heal was as important as their duty to preach. "Then he called his twelve disciples together, and gave them power and authority over all devils, and to cure diseases. And he sent them to preach the kingdom of God, and to heal the sick. . . ." *(Luke 9)*.

The disciples retained the ability to heal after Jesus' death. These miraculous cures greatly contributed to the spread of Christianity. The Apostles and their successors healed by the laying on of hands and calling on the name of Jesus, and in the eyes of the many suffering people, this was what distinguished Christianity from other religions and current ideas. In Greek mystery cults, for example, the body was regarded as no more than a prison of the soul, unworthy of special regard. But the early Church was concerned with the health and salvation of both body and soul.

One of the greatest contributions of the early Christians was the foundation of hospitals. Caring for the sick and needy was seen as an essential part of Christian life, and as a way of carrying out Christ's healing mission. Christian hospitals played such an important part in the life of the community that when the Emperor Julian the Apostate tried to restore the worship of the pagan gods in the 4th century, he set up rival hospitals to gain popularity for his beliefs. However, these failed.

All kinds of illnesses were treated by prayer and the laying on of hands. There are many stories of the cures of people who were mentally sick, or possessed by demons as it was then termed. In the 4th century, a young boy who was thought to be possessed by an evil spirit was brought by his father to the saintly hermit Macarius, who lived in the Egyptian desert. Putting one hand on the boy's head and the other on his heart, Macarius began to pray. Gradually the boy's body started to swell up until it seemed as if he were suspended in the air. Suddenly he gave a cry. Water poured from his body, which then returned to its normal shape. The boy was cured.

Records of healing abound in the early Church. Rites were devised for visiting, anointing, and laying hands upon the sick. These actions were performed not only by the priests, but also by the laity—by servants as well as saints. Sometimes cures were achieved by communal prayer. Gorgonia, sister of the 4th–century saint Gregory of Nazianzus, was dragged over the ground

by a team of mules, and so badly injured that her life was despaired of. She was cured by the prayers of the congregation. By the 4th century, however, it is clear from many writers that despite remarkable cures by many individual figures, the healing ministry of the Church had started to decline. The conversion to Christianity of the Roman Emperor Constantine in A.D. 313 had ended the Christian persecutions, but had flooded the Church with token Christians. The Church lost its missionary thrust and turned its energies inward to fighting heresies. Christianity was still not short of saints or holy men, however. St. Augustine performed several remarkable cures, and so did St. Ambrose in Milan and St. Martin of Tours, who was best known for his act of cutting his cloak in half to share it with a beggar. But cures were becoming rarer. The crumbling of civilization before the onslaught of the barbarians led to a general turning away from the pain of this world to the hoped-for glories of the next. This is well illustrated in the changing use of the ceremony of anointing with oil, known as *unction*.

The early Christians anointed the sick with oil, following this famous passage in Chapter 5 of St. James's Epistle: "Is there any sick among you? Let him call for the elders of the church; and let them pray over him, anointing with oil in the name of the Lord."

Above: Christ healing the blind man at Bethsaida, from an 11th-century Italian painting. It shows the man being anointed with some clay, and later washing his eyes at the pool of Siloam where he discovered he could see.

63

Above: this late 15th-century French miniature shows a priest sprinkling a dying man with holy water during the rite of Extreme Unction. By this time the original purpose of unction—which was anointing a sick person with oil as a cure—had been entirely transformed into a sacrament for the dying. The painting also depicts how the soul of the dying person is being snatched away from the devil. Bodleian Library, Oxford (MS Liturg. 41, f. 147).

Members of the sick person's congregation would gather in his or her house together with several priests—sometimes as many as seven. The rooms would be sprinkled with a mixture of salt and holy water, and prayers would be spoken. If the sick individual were strong enough, he would kneel for the laying on of hands and the anointing. Oil would be applied to the throat, back, and breast, and more liberally where the pain was felt most severely. The ceremony could be repeated as often as was thought necessary.

By the 8th century the emphasis had shifted. Oil was no longer applied to the appropriate part of the body. The idea that sickness was God's punishment for sin was uppermost, and the sick were ritually anointed to indicate the five senses through which mankind commits sin. A hair shirt was spread on the floor, and the sick person was placed on it. A sign of the cross was marked on him in ashes to remind him of his eventual end. The emphasis was no longer on healing but on repentance, a preparation for the next world rather than recovery in this.

Later its use changed even more radically. It became known as Extreme Unction and was administered only to those about to die. By medieval times the original purpose of the ceremony had been so far forgotten that if a person recovered after receiving Extreme Unction, he was still regarded as legally dead. He was not allowed to marry, nor could he alter his will.

The neglect of the healing ministry of Jesus represented a great loss for the Church and for humanity generally. Throughout the centuries powerful personalities with the gift of healing occasion-

Above: three miracles from the
life of Saint Zenobius, by
Botticelli. On the left he
exorcises two young men cursed
with gnawing their own flesh;
in the center he brings a
noblewoman's son back to life;
and at the right he restores
the sight of a blind beggar.
These miracles, so closely
paralleling events in the life
of Christ, were typical of the
miracles attributed to many of
the early Christian saints.

ally appeared, and it is significant that these nearly always
represented forces for religious renewal. In the 12th century St.
Francis of Assisi and St. Bernard of Clairvaux achieved many
cures. St. Catherine of Siena in the 14th century and St. Francis
Xavier in the 16th century were renowned for their healing
power. George Fox, who founded the Society of Friends, or
Quakers, in the 17th century, performed many cures both in
England and America. Fox never published his *Book of Miracles*
in which he kept notes of his cures, fearing that it would expose
the struggling young Quaker movement to further mockery and
persecution. Yet while the English of his day seized any opportunity to laugh at a cure worked by a man of God, they flocked in
their thousands—even paying money for tickets—to see the

Right: the head of Saint Francis
Xavier photographed in 1974,
423 years after his death. In
life he was a renowned healer,
and miracles of healing have
been reported by people who
touched his body or its casket.
The body itself mysteriously
failed to decay until the 1970s,
400 years after he died.

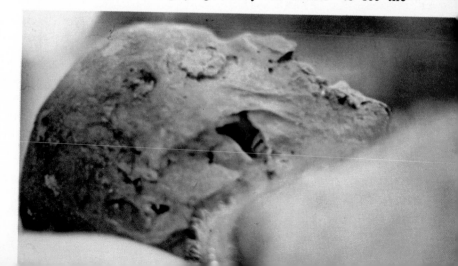

Right: Charles II touching a sufferer of the King's Evil, or scrofula. The tradition of the king's healing powers in England go back to Edward the Confessor, who died in the year of the Norman Conquest. Edward, however, touched for a variety of ailments. Later, scrofula was the only illness that the king was believed to be able to cure.

Above: King Henry IV of France touching for *Le Mal Royal*. There is considerable evidence for supposing that the king's touch as a cure for scrofula began in France, and that William the Conqueror brought it to England.

dissolute King Charles II try to cure scrofula by his touch. Scrofula, a tubercular affliction of the glands of the neck, was known popularly as the "king's evil."

There had long been pagan rulers who possessed healing powers. King Pyrrhus of Epirus in the 3rd century B.C. cured colic by the unusual practice of the laying on of *toes*. But there was no record of the healing power of Christian kings until the 11th century, when King Robert the Pious of France and King Edward the Confessor in England cured cases of scrofula by placing their hands on the necks of the sick and making the sign of the cross.

Why scrofula was singled out to be the royal disease is not known, but the supposed power of kings to cure it became hereditary with the English and French thrones, and reached phenomenal popularity in the 17th century. The sufferers were brought before the king who blessed them, touched their sores, and gave them a coin to hang around their necks. Since these coins in England were generally gold angels, the cost to the treasury was high. Charles II extravagantly touched 90,798 sufferers in 19 years. However, William III touched only one person, and that reluctantly. "God give you better health," he said, "and more sense." Queen Anne was the last English monarch to practice touching.

It seems to be the case that as one method of healing declines another develops to take its place. As touch-healing among the early Christians gradually diminished, the use of relics of the saints and martyrs became more widespread.

As early as the time of St. Paul handkerchiefs and aprons belonging to the Apostle were being pressed against the sick, and it is recorded that "the disease departed from them." But the practice of using the material remains of a saint, or some object sanctified by contact with his body, did not become widespread until the conversion of Constantine marked the end of the Christian persecutions. It then became safe to dig up the remains of the martyrs and reinter them in newly built churches. Cures were effected by the relics of St. Stephen, the first Christian martyr, by Sts. Cosmas and Damian, the physician brothers of the 3rd century, and by numerous others. In Rome the body of St. Sebastian was particularly treasured because of the circumstances of his death. The archers of the emperor had been unable to kill him although they shot his body so full of arrows that, according to the legend, he looked like a hedgehog. Darts and arrows had always symbolized sudden death, and Sebastian's ability to survive them made him a patron saint of the sick.

Many tombs became shrines at which the sick went to pray and pass the night by the remains of the entombed saint within. The builders of Chartres Cathedral in the 12th century designed the crypt so that it could be washed down after the sick pilgrims had left. Reliquaries of great beauty were fashioned to house fragments of the True Cross and other relics of the Passion of Jesus. King Louis IX of France, who became St. Louis, built the exquisite Sainte-Chapelle in Paris to honor the Crown of Thorns he had brought back from Constantinople.

One of the most celebrated healings associated with a relic of Jesus is the cure of Marguerite Perier, a niece of the French philosopher and mathematician Blaise Pascal. She was a young novice nun who had suffered for three years from a fistula in her eye. On March 25, 1646 she approached the altar rails to kneel and kiss a thorn from the Crown of Thorns. The nun in charge, feeling distressed at the terrible condition of the girl's eye, acted on a sudden impulse. She touched the sore with the relic. A quarter of an hour later the pus had stopped running, the ulcer had dried up, and Marguerite Perier was cured. Pascal was so moved by the event that he added to his armorial bearings an eye surrounded by a crown of thorns, with the Latin motto *Scio cui credidi*, "What I once believed, I now know."

The Virgin Mary was not given any significant role by the Christian Church in the early years. By the 4th century, however, people had begun to pray to Mary to intercede for them in times of sickness and difficulty. Her popularity with the mass of the people increased so rapidly that the veneration accorded her in the Middle Ages sometimes seemed to outstrip that given to Christ. Many churches were dedicated to her and many shrines

Above: a George III touchpiece, made of silver. It was part of the touching ceremony that the king would bestow a coin upon the sufferer—first a penny and later a much more valuable one.

Above: the hand of Saint Attale in a reliquary. In Roman Catholic tradition a relic is regarded as a means of communion with a saint, giving something physical to fix the mind on. In the Middle Ages, however, relics became worshipped as objects of power in themselves, and miracles of healing were ascribed to them.

were built in her honor. In Spain the Black Madonna of Montserrat near Barcelona draws the sick to this day, but the most famous of all shrines dedicated to the Virgin is Lourdes in the French Pyrenees.

The story of Lourdes started on a February day in 1858. Bernadette Soubirous, the asthmatic daughter of a poverty-stricken miller, went out with other children of the village to gather driftwood from the river. In a shallow grotto on the river bank the vision of "a lady" came to her. The vision returned at intervals over the next few months, and finally identified itself by saying to Bernadette in the local dialect the girl spoke, "I am the Immaculate Conception." (The belief that the Virgin Mary had been conceived immaculately—that is to say, free from original sin—had recently been proclaimed a dogma by the Pope.) Bernadette was led by her vision to a spring that no one knew existed in the back of the cave. Not long after, the first cures were reported by villagers who tried the waters of the spring.

At that time the Catholic Church was sensitive to accusations that it pandered to the credulity of peasants. Neither the Church nor the local authorities wanted a miracle on their hands, and the grotto was boarded up. Before long, however, the boards were taken down on the express orders of Napoleon III, and in 1862 a Church Commission of Enquiry confirmed that Bernadette's vision had taken place. The cures resumed and have continued ever since, though now the spring water is piped to especially constructed baths where the pilgrims can be immersed.

By the 1870s great pilgrimages were arriving at the shrine on a scale unlike anything seen since the crusades. In 1876 a huge white basilica was constructed above the rock, and a marble statue of the Virgin was placed in the cave where Bernadette had seen her lady. So many cures were claimed that the Church authorities were obliged to set up a Medical Bureau to try to sort out the genuine cures. The system was reorganized in 1947, and today the sick are given an examination on their arrival at Lourdes. They are also expected to bring with them a diagnosis from their own doctors. When a patient reports a cure, he is examined at the Bureau. Visiting doctors can also attend this examination. The patient must return a year later for further examination if still well. If the Bureau is satisfied that the cure is both unexplained and permanent, the case is forwarded to a higher medical tribunal in Paris. Finally, it must go before the members of an ecclesiastical tribunal, who may declare the cure to be miraculous. They may also decide that, while being genuine, it is for certain reasons, nonmiraculous.

The conditions imposed by the tribunals are strict, and the proportion of authenticated cures is not high. Between two and three million pilgrims now visit Lourdes annually, but in just over a hundred years of the shrine, fewer than 60 miracles have been proclaimed. Even in the nonmiraculous though still genuine category of cures, the number is not above 6000. One of the accepted cures was of an Irishman, Charles Macdonald. He had been an invalid for four years and confined to his bed for nearly 18 months. The tuberculosis which had attacked him in his early twenties had spread from his lungs to his spine, left shoulder, and kidneys. At the age of 31, as he was about to be admitted to

Dublin's Hospice for the Dying, he decided to make the pilgrimage to Lourdes.

The morning after his arrival he received Holy Communion, and was taken to join the long line of invalids slowly making its way to the Grotto. He was lifted from his stretcher and put onto another one made of webbing, and especially constructed for use at the baths. It was hoisted above the bath, and after the prayers and invocations, was lowered into the icy water. For Macdonald, the shock of the first immersion was a terrible experience. It is customary for invalids to undergo two immersions on two successive days, and Macdonald awaited the second one with dread. However, it was not nearly as bad as he had anticipated, and to his astonishment, he found that when he was replaced on his stretcher, the pain always present in the last few years had vanished. He could relax without discomfort, and almost sit up.

Macdonald spent the rest of the day in a state of terror about what had happened. The next morning he got out of bed by himself and walked around the Grotto twice. He was able to travel back to Dublin without the aid of a stretcher. A year later the Lourdes doctors reached the conclusion that "no medical explanation in the actual state of existing science could explain the extraordinary rapidity of this cure." They decided that it was clearly outside ordinary biological law.

Strangely, the patient's faith does not always play a part in the Lourdes cures. The case of Louis Olivari illustrates this. Olivari was a French Communist, an electrician and frustrated local politician. His body was paralyzed down one side because of a fall from a ladder. His wife had urged him many times to go to Lourdes, but he had always refused because he was opposed to everything it stood for. When she finally persuaded him to go in

Left: Saint Sebastian pierced by the arrows which, according to tradition, failed to kill him because of his deep faith. His body was a particular relic for the church in Rome, and his ability to survive despite wounds that should have killed him made him a patron saint of the sick.

Above: Marguerite Perier and the Crown of Thorns—still a relic in the Cathedral of Notre Dame in Paris—which miraculously cured her of a fistula in her eye. After her sister nun had impulsively touched her eye with the Crown, the ulcer had completely healed within a quarter of an hour.

JE SUIS L'IMMACULEE CONCEPTION
U. L. FRAU VON LOURDES

Left: Bernadette Soubirous in 1858. She was the asthmatic daughter of a shiftless miller, and had difficulty in learning her catechism. But through years of cross-examination, even after she became a nun, she clung to her story of the lady in the grotto. She died of asthma and a tumor at the age of 35, refusing to go to the waters that were then curing so many of the faithful. Below: the grotto of Lourdes as it appeared by the middle 1870s.

Above: a religious postcard of 1867, showing the apparition of Lourdes. It was only nine years after Bernadette's vision, but by then the mysterious cures had already begun at the shrine.

the summer of 1956, he watched the dipping and praying in a spirit of some cynicism. The place was exactly as he had expected. Among the pilgrims was a young blind boy making his fifth visit. He became aware that Olivari was holding himself aloof, and called out to him "Pray!" Olivari found himself moved by this appeal, and as his turn came to be dipped he cried out, "God, if you exist, cure this boy who deserves it more than I do." As he spoke these words he felt faint. He had to be pulled from the water. When he was placed on the ground once more, he found that he was no longer paralyzed. He could walk.

As can be seen from its treatment of Lourdes, the Catholic Church is cautious in its attitude to miracle healing. Certain individuals with the gift of healing have in the past been discouraged because of their extreme behavior. One of these was Johann Joseph Gassner, born in 1727 in Austria. He became a priest, but his continued ill health interfered with his parochial duties. He noticed, to his surprise, that his various pains increased while he was celebrating mass. He decided that the Devil was trying to get possession of him, and began to practice a kind of self-exorcism. His health improved, and he came to the conclusion that many illnesses were caused by interference from the Devil. Some years later he began to attempt to heal others by casting out demons. He used a shortened form of exorcism of his own invention, and under the patronage of the Bishop of Regensburg treated about 2000 sufferers a month. Not content with this success, he organized mass meetings at which patients carried out his commands to laugh, cry, fall into a trance, or reproduce an epileptic fit. Gassner had obviously discovered something important about the relationship of the mind to the body, but his showmanship and unorthodoxy was his undoing. He was soon forbidden to practice by the Church.

A more fortunate Catholic healer was Prince Alexander Leopold Franz Emmerich von Hohenlohe-Waldenburg-Schillingfürst. Born in Würtemburg in 1794, he became a priest. At the age of 27 he discovered he could often cure the sick by praying with them, laying hands on them, or simply commanding them to be well. His aristocratic birth afforded him a certain protection but he still came under pressure, especially from the medical profession, to abandon his contact healing. No authority could

Left: pilgrims attending mass in front of the chapel at Lourdes. Each year more than two million people visit this French shrine, either in hope of a cure or to share its extraordinary atmosphere of faith and consolation.

Above right: the sick making their way to the grotto. Even the very ill are bathed in the cold waters of Lourdes, and although many of their ailments are infectious, tradition has it that no one has ever fallen ill after being in the spring.

Right: the grotto of Lourdes today. Even in the cold dawn at 5:30 those hopeful of a cure are already at their prayers.

prevent him from praying for the sick, however. In 1821 he let it be known that at certain hours of the day he would be offering up a special mass for the sick, and urged those who were ill to join with him in prayer at the same time. Those who wrote to him would be named in his prayers. Prince von Hohenlohe thus became the first practitioner of "absent healing" in modern times.

From his church in Bamberg in Bavaria he treated a young novice nun who lived near Chelmsford, England. Infection from a poisoned thumb had spread to her arm and shoulder, and her wrist had swollen to a circumference of 15 inches. Eighteen months of medical treatment had been of no use. Finally one day the surgeons advised amputation. However, the following day von Hohenlohe mentioned the girl by name in one of his special masses. It was later confirmed that at the time his service, conducted over a thousand miles away, was due to end, the swelling of the young nun's arm had begun to diminish. By that evening the wrist measured only five inches. In four days the girl was cured.

An even more remarkable cure took place in the United States on March 10, 1824. The sister of the Mayor of Washington was desperately ill, and on the brink of death. She was suffering from almost total paralysis. It had been decided to ask von Hohenlohe to attempt absent healing. A mass was celebrated at the invalid's bedside at 3:30 a.m. in order to coincide with the European hour of the Mass being celebrated by von Hohenlohe. The *Catholic Spectator* reported what occurred, saying:

"At the moment of receiving the Blessed Sacrament (which her tongue being quite parched and dead-like, she could hardly effect) she rises up in her bed, and lifting up her two arms, one of which she had not been able for a long time even to move, she exclaims—"Lord Jesus, what have I done to obtain so great a favor? What shall I do to acknowledge so great a benefit?", asks for her clothes, dresses herself, sits up, throws herself down on her knees with the priest, the Rev. Stephen Dubuisson, who had given her the holy communion, and who was prostrate on the ground, lost in a transport of admiration and gratitude, then rises, walks through the room, and on that same morning took as much food as she had taken for the space of six months previous...."

That day she received a thousand visitors, and the following day two thousand. She shook hands with them all to the astonishment of her physicians. From the "ghastly, emaciated, livid semblance of a dying person" she was "restored to an angelical countenance."

The United States in the 19th century was a fertile breeding ground for healing cults. Among the many that are forgotten now, save as curiosities, is the "harmonial philosophy" of

A Double Miracle at Lourdes

Josephine Hoare, a healthy girl of 21, had been married for only six months when she developed chronic *nephritis*, a serious inflammation of the kidneys. Her family was told that she had no more than two years to live. At her mother's suggestion, she was taken to Lourdes.

At the famous French shrine, Josephine braved the icy waters of the spring. Although she felt peaceful, she was not conscious of any change. When she went home, however, her doctor said in amazement that the disorder seemed to have cleared. Her swollen legs returned to normal size, her blood pressure became normal, and her energy increased. But she was warned that pregnancy would certainly cause a relapse.

Several years passed. Then Josephine and her husband had the opportunity to revisit Lourdes, and Josephine lit a candle of thanksgiving. Soon after they got home, she felt a sharp pain in her back. Fearful that nephritis was recurring, she went to her doctor. His diagnosis was simply that she was six months pregnant—and she had had no relapse.

Josephine Hoare had her baby, a son, and remained in good health. For her and her family, the spring of Lourdes had produced a double miracle.

Right: a collection of medals and postcard souvenirs from pilgrimages, among them some of Lourdes, Prague, and Paris. Although there are other shrines that the sick visit, Lourdes still remains the most popular.

Above: a religious postcard of the 20th century depicts Saint Teresa of Lisieux undergoing a miraculous cure by the Virgin Mary. Saint Teresa, who died of tuberculosis at the age of 24, is noted for her simple devotion and faithful attention to the many tiresome little daily duties.

Andrew Jackson Davis. He at first worked as a mesmerist, diagnosing and curing people's ailments while in a trance state. His writings and theories helped to establish the Spiritualist movement, and it was while in a trance that he dictated one of his many lengthy books expounding his theory that there is no such thing as mind, only matter. Christian Science, also founded in the 19th century, took the opposing view that spirit was the only true reality. However, whereas many healing movements had short-term success and then faded away, Christian Science grew and expanded into one of the most important healing movements in history. Many of its cures have baffled medical experts. Here is one of its early successes.

In 1886 in East Windsor, Connecticut, Joseph Mann was

accidentally shot by his brother-in-law while engaged in target practice. The young man of 22, one of a large and devoted family, was carried unconscious and bleeding heavily into the house. When the family doctor saw how serious the wound was he immediately summoned three more of the town's most skillful and conscientious physicians. However, after long and careful examination of the injury and much worried consultation, they told the agonized family that there was nothing they could do to save Joseph's life. From the excessive bleeding and strange color of the blood, they concluded that the bullet must have touched the heart, and that even if they were able to stem the external flow of blood the patient would still bleed to death internally. The family doctor remained with the grieving relatives until death had begun to set in. As he left them he told them there was no hope. The body had begun to grow cold, the eyes were becoming set, and the pulse was scarcely perceptible. In despair the family began to prepare telegrams to inform friends of the sad news.

Just at this time a Christian Scientist came to visit and asked to be allowed to see the patient. The family knew nothing about Christian Science, but finally agreed on condition that nothing was done to disturb the dying man. About a quarter of an hour after the Christian Scientist had entered Joseph began to grow warm again. His breath started to come normally. He gradually regained consciousness. That very evening he sat up in bed and ate some steak and toast. The excruciating pain lessened.

The astonished doctors direly predicted that gangrene would set in, but although nothing was done to the wound except washing it, the patient continued to improve. The following day he was up and out of bed, and the third day it seemed as if the accident had never occurred. The gratitude of the family to Christian Science was boundless. Three brothers, including Joseph, and two sisters became active in the Christian Science movement, and began to spread its teachings.

Christian Science is both a religious faith and a way of life. For its founder, Mary Baker Eddy, it represented a return to the early truths of Christianity, in particular Christian healing.

In 1866 Mary Baker Eddy, then Mrs. Patterson, had slipped and fallen on some ice in Lynn, Massachusetts. She was then 45 years old, and weak from a life of debilitating illness and personal tragedy. It was feared that she had suffered fatal internal injuries. While she was reading the Bible and praying she underwent a sudden religious experience that was to change her life and the lives of many others. She had a revelation of life in and of Spirit, totally separate from the world of matter. She was cured immediately, and able to walk again. This experience led to her discovery of what she came to understand as the Science of Christianity, or Christian Science.

In 1875 she published the first version of *Science and Health*, the book that after many revisions by the author was, with the Bible, to form the basis of the Christian Science movement.

In 1879 the first Christian Science church was founded near Boston and by early 1975 there were some 3100 churches and societies in 57 countries around the world.

Like their founder, Christian Scientists hold that humanity's aim must be to overcome the illusions of the world, which include

Below: Alexander Leopold, the Prince of Hohenlohe-Waldenburg-Schillingfürst (1794–1849). He became a priest and, discovering that he had the gift of healing, began to perform cures by the laying on of hands. When this aroused Church protest, he found he could heal simply by prayer, even if the patient was far away.

Above: Phineas Parkhurst Quimby, the healer who first showed Mrs. Mary Baker Eddy, founder of Christian Science, that it was possible to cure a sick person by the power of faith alone.

Below: Mary Baker Eddy. A woman of strong personality, she made herself well through self-treatment and faith. Her belief that disease can be driven from the body by the power of the mind is still the cornerstone of the Christian Science movement.

sickness, pain, and even death. Jesus' cures are seen not as miracles but as the natural result of his understanding of God, and his boundless love for humanity. Christian Scientists believe that healing takes place when, through prayer, God dispels suffering from the consciousness of the individual.

The 20th century has seen the emergence of an astonishing number of healers. Their variety is no less remarkable. They range from those who try to avoid publicity to those who employ the most up-to-date techniques to advertise their skills. There are devout Catholic priests and no less devout Protestant evangelists. The much respected Padre Pio, parish priest in the South Italian town of Foggia, remained in his remote hometown hearing the confessions of his parishioners, and curing with prayers the pilgrims who undertook the journey to him. In striking contrast, the Reverend Oral Roberts toured the United States conducting healing services in a vast tent, and spread his message through regular radio broadcasts.

In South Africa Mrs. Elsie Salmon, wife of a Methodist minister, placed her hands as "directed" by Jesus and felt the healing power flow through her to the patient like a current of electricity. The Polish-born Madame Sikora regarded sickness as a fever she could draw out from a patient, and she interrupted her treatments from time to time to flick her hands at a corner of the room as though shaking water from her fingers.

The American Presbyterian Professor Wade Boggs has tried to establish the principle by which faith healing works, but has found a great deal of variation. "Sometimes," he explains, "these cures are attributed directly to the healing power of God. Again the faith of a sick man, and of his friends, is said to play a part. Prayer is considered essential by many. Value is often attributed to such means as sacramental oil, or the laying on of hands. . . . Others attribute healing power to the guidance of spirits, others to the Virgin Mary, others to the relics of dead saints. The theories behind these healing movements vary widely and in fact are often radically opposed to one another."

It may be that the underlying principle of faith healing was isolated nearly 70 years ago by the Reverend Edward Worcester when he described the pioneering Emmanuel Movement he had founded in Boston. He achieved considerable success in curing tuberculosis by taking patients out of the slums and treating them with rest, fresh air, and prayer. The city health authorities decided to follow suit—but did not include the prayers. Lacking this component they achieved nothing. Success, suggested Dr. Worcester, "rests upon the recognition of powers within the soul of man of which we were not formally aware."

The faith healer taps the sources of this power. The faith of the patient is concentrated on something which of itself may have no power to heal, but this concentration releases the body's own power to heal itself.

How this principle works is still far from being understood. In many cases it fails to work; but in many other cases—as tens of thousands of cured people can testify—the power of faith heals.

Right: Padre Pio, a Capuchin monk in a remote Italian village, was credited with many cures by prayer alone before his death in 1968.

5

Spirits and Ghosts

"His psychological terms and description of the nervous anatomy would do credit to any professor of nervous anatomy. There is no faltering in his speech and all his statements are clear and concise. He handles the most complex jawbreakers with as much ease as any Boston physician, which to me is quite wonderful, in view of the fact that while in his normal state he is an illiterate man, especially along the line of medicine, surgery or pharmacy, of which he knows nothing."

This description of Edgar Cayce, perhaps the most celebrated psychic diagnostician of modern times, was given by a skilled and successful doctor who worked alongside him

The power of the human spirit—even after the body confining it has died—to heal others is a proven fact to many who would cite the experience of spiritual healers all around the world. Right: Mrs. Olive Burton, an assistant to the British spirit healer Harry Edwards, works to restore a patient's vision at the Edwards' Healing Sanctuary.

"It became apparent that Cayce had certain psychic faculties"

for many years, using the guidance Cayce gave while in trance to help him treat his most intractable cases. One of these was a college boy, the son of a wealthy family. For no apparent reason he had suddenly gone out of his mind. He could only mutter a few words, was prone to violent seizures, and otherwise would sit speechless, staring in front of him for hours on end. With money no object, his distraught parents consulted specialists from all over the country. His condition was pronounced hopeless and deteriorating. When Cayce was given his name and address—the only information he ever required about a patient—and went into trance, he diagnosed the boy's illness and prescribed a little-known drug. The drug was administered —and within a month the boy had recovered.

Edgar Cayce was born in Hopkinsville, Kentucky in 1877. He received almost no formal education. As he grew up it became apparent that he had certain psychic faculties. However, it was not until his early twenties, when he came into contact with a hypnotist named Al Layne, that he himself recognized the full extent of his own extraordinary powers. Cayce suffered from a severe throat condition that doctors had been unable to cure. Layne took the unusual step of putting him to sleep, and then telling him to diagnose his own complaint. From his trance Edgar Cayce began his own diagnosis with the words, "Yes we can see the body," a phrase that was to be repeated thousands of times in his subsequent work. He went on in a clear voice to pinpoint his own trouble as partial paralysis of the vocal chords, and to suggest that the problem could be cured by an increase of blood circulation in the area for a short time. Still in trance, Cayce used self-hypnosis to cause the circulation to be increased at that particular point, and then to return to normal. In a few moments he came round. He remembered nothing, but his voice was restored.

Layne, who had been ill for years, then persuaded Cayce to diagnose him, although Cayce was still unconvinced of his own ability. From his trance state Cayce was able to describe all Layne's symptoms, and prescribe treatment in medical terms that in his waking state he was unable to understand. It seemed as if some strange power were talking through him. Later he was to demonstrate, in trance, knowledge of languages and of scientific and historical facts that in his conscious mind he knew nothing of. When he began to give regular readings, as his trance diagnoses were called, he usually had someone skilled in medicine present to make sure that none of the remedies he prescribed in his readings were harmful.

Because of attempts to exploit his clairvoyant powers in order to make money, Cayce also insisted that his wife be present at all sessions to supervise the questions put to him. He would lie down on a couch, having loosened his collar, cuffs, and laces. His wife would touch his cheek, and he would close his eyes and begin to breathe deeply. His wife and his secretary would close their eyes in prayer, and then Mrs. Cayce would initiate the reading by giving him the name and address of the subject. Cayce would then visualize the state of health of the subject, wherever he was, and also his surroundings. In recommending treatment Cayce would often direct patients to therapists or doctors whom he did not know outside his trance condition. One Staten Island mother, consulting him for a sick child, was told to "Find Dobbins." Eventually she traced a young osteopath named Frank Dobbins who had just arrived in Staten Island, and whose name was not yet in the phone directory. Cayce had never heard of him nor he of Cayce.

The prescriptions Cayce gave while in trance were often incomprehensible to a pharmacist. They contained a strange mixture of ingredients of which some were totally unfamiliar. Sometimes the unusual ingredients were not yet on the market. Other times they were substances that had fallen out of use. At one time Cayce prescribed balsam of sulphur. The druggists who were to fill the prescription were unable to find it in any current list of therapeutic drugs. Finally they unearthed from an attic a 50-year-old catalog. In this they found balsam of sulphur mentioned. On another occasion Cayce recommended the use of clary water for rheumatism. As no druggist had ever heard of it, the patient advertised for anyone who could give any information on the subject. A man from Paris replied that his father had developed the product, but that it had been out of use for nearly 50 years. He enclosed a copy of the original prescription. Without prior knowledge of this prescription, Cayce asked himself in a trance state how clary water could be made. His answer tallied exactly with the original directions.

As his fame grew he was inundated with requests for help, and a fully staffed hospital was set up for him in Virginia Beach. In 1931 the Association for Research and Enlightenment began to keep records of the thousands of cases he had treated. Although Cayce died in 1945, his readings on file at the Association continue to be studied for the insight they give into the treatment and diagnosis of illness, and many followers of Cayce carry out the ideas he put forward while in trance.

How could he do it? And if he could do it, could anyone? These are the kinds of questions that present themselves time and again in the world of spirit healing. Strictly speaking Cayce, who has been called the outstanding sensitive of the century, was a diagnostician and not a healer. He did not possess in himself the power to cure, but his psychic perceptions showed the way back to health for thousands who consulted him.

Many modern faith healers are Spiritualists. Why is this so? Spiritualists believe that the human personality outlives the death of the physical body, a belief they share with most of the world's great and small religions. But Spiritualists go further in believing that the spirits of the dead can and do communicate with the living.

The Ancient Egyptians feared the spirits of the dead as envious bringers of disease. Among the California and Oregon Indians a strict tribal law forbade the speaking of any person's name after his death for fear it brought back his ghost. In parts of Indonesia some names given to people were also the names of common objects such as "fowl" and "fire." With the death of a man who bore such a name, the name of the object had to be changed. This led to great difficulties in communication.

All these measures were designed to protect the living from the dead. Spiritualists, on the other hand, believe that the dead,

Above: Edward Cayce and his wife Gertrude. Lacking formal education, Cayce found himself capable of producing amazingly detailed facts about illness and successful remedies when in trance. Now, 30 years after his death, the records of his diagnoses are still being used by doctors to decide how to treat their patients.

far from harming us, want to help us. The spirits of those who have died retain their human personality, and seek out the opportunity to return to earth and continue their work.

To return to the physical plane, the spirits normally require the agency of a sensitive intermediary, a medium who can serve as a junction and channel between the two worlds. Prominent among those who seek to return, it seems, are men who practiced healing when they were alive. Many of the Chinese and Indian spirit guides that featured strongly in early Spiritualist lore are thought to have been physicians or medicine men knowledgeable in healing arts unfamiliar to Western man. Harry Edwards, the most celebrated contemporary British healer, believes the spirits of Louis Pasteur and Lord Lister direct his work.

Edwards' first healings occurred in the Middle East during World War I when he was in charge of a crew of Arabs building a railroad. They were inexperienced laborers, and accidents were frequent. Those who smashed their fingers with hammers found their wounds healed unexpectedly quickly if Edwards treated them. He attributed this to the hardiness of their race, but they recognized his unusual power and called him the *hakim*—healer. Edwards returned from the war believing his gift was nothing special, and for the next 15 years concentrated on the family's printing business. Not until 1935 when he was

Above: the Blackheath Center of Healing and Meditation, one of Britain's Spiritualist healing groups in the London area. Ron Eager, shown speaking, founded the group after he himself was cured of epilepsy and colitis.

Right: healing by the laying on of hands at the Blackheath Center by Eager and an assistant trained by him. The little girl, whose throat was swollen by tonsillitis, was completely cured of her throat and related ear troubles in a week.

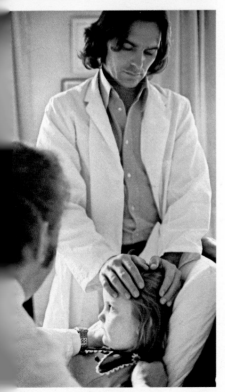

over 40, did he turn his attention to Spiritualism and healing.

As an amateur conjuror his interest was at first limited to reproducing Spiritualistic phenomena by trickery. But he soon decided there was more to Spiritualism. Mediums at several of the Spiritualist circles he attended told him he was "born to heal," and a succession of events gradually persuaded him that he did in fact possess the healing gift. In one instance he and two friends were sitting quietly in meditation one day concentrating their thoughts on a man they knew to be in London's Brompton Hospital. He was dying of advanced tuberculosis. Edwards became aware that he was gazing down a long hospital ward with his attention fixed on a man in the last bed but one. When he afterward checked what he had "seen" with someone who had visited the patient, he discovered his description was accurate in every detail. It was Edwards' first experience of astral traveling.

Within a day of his vision, the friend's hemorrhage ceased and his temperature was almost down to normal. He recovered and remained in good health for many years.

Convinced by this and other like experiences that he could be used as a medium for healing, Edwards began to follow the Spiritualist healing methods then in use. He soon found, however, that it was unnecessary for him to go into trance as most Spiritualist healers did. The spirit guides seemed to work through him just as well when he was in a state of receptive meditation. Sometimes he would just sit and let the healing force flow through him to a sufferer, perhaps many hundreds of miles away. At other times he might feel moved to manipulate the arthritic joints of a patient. Till well into his 70s, Edwards held large public demonstrations of healing at which sufferers from disabilities such as rheumatism, curvature of the spine, and paralysis would come forward to be helped or cured by him and his team of assistants. As his successes became more and more widely known, so his mail increased, until thousands of letters began to pour in every year with requests for absent healing. Edwards came to believe that absent healing, often without the patient's knowledge, was more effective than direct healing.

At one time Edwards felt his duties should include convincing the medical and church authorities that spiritual healing worked. He gathered details of several hundred cases, and provided X-ray data and surgeons' reports. He placed special hopes on their being finally convinced by the cases of Mr. R. B., cured of cancer in 1953.

This was a case in which it had been proved by a *biopsy*, which is the medical term for the removal and examination of a small portion of the tissue thought to be diseased, that Mr. B. was suffering from a malignant cancerous condition of the throat. All the usual symptoms were present. He had severe pain and swelling, he was unable to swallow, and his voice had deteriorated into a hoarse whisper. He was due to be operated on in two weeks.

When Mr. B. learned of this decision he telephoned Edwards for absent healing. "In the immediate days following," Edwards says, "the pains left him and the swellings subsided; and his

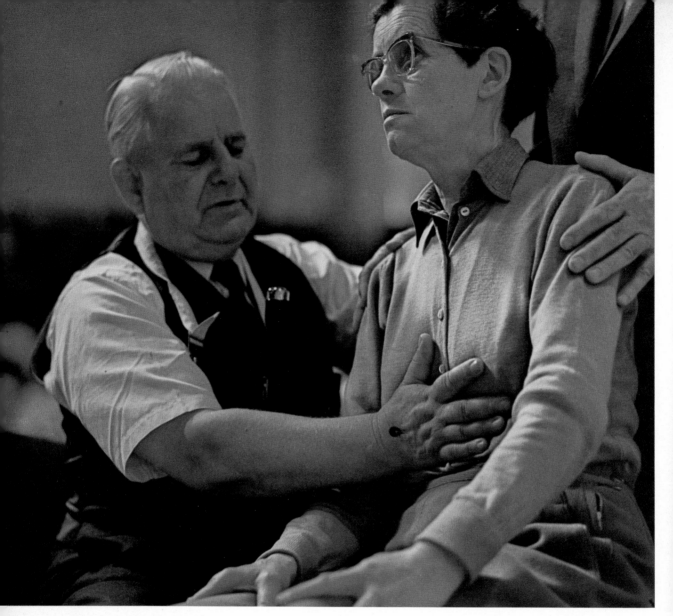

Above: Harry Edwards treating a patient at an open demonstration of his healing powers, held in the north of England in 1964.

voice returned to normal." Two days before the operation was due to take place Mr. B. requested a further examination by the two specialists who had conducted the previous examinations. "After exhaustive tests and a fresh biopsy, they declared that all symptoms of the cancer had disappeared."

This seemed to Edwards proof enough that a cure by spirit healing had occurred. But the two specialists disputed this. Their explanation was that by a fortunate coincidence the section of tissue removed for the first examination contained all the diseased tissue.

As a result of experiences like this Edwards decided against further attempts to prove spirit healing. The proof that mattered was to be found in the healings themselves—healings, incidentally, for which Edwards himself takes no credit. "I myself have never 'cured' anyone," he says. "My part is simply that of a channel for the healing powers."

As to how these powers operate, the British healer Gordon Turner has put forward some ideas in his book *An Outline of Spiritual Healing*, published in 1963. It is based on his study of the *aura*, a field of energy believed to surround all living creatures. Turner possesses considerable psychic powers. He has described the aura around an ant's nest as a faintly pinkish glow, becoming darker around the body of each ant. A pet budgerigar was surrounded by a faint blue light about twice the size of the bird's body. The aura that surrounds a human body is necessarily more complex. Turner sees it as an ever-changing pattern of rippling color, densest where close to the physical body and faintest at the outer edge. Emotions are registered in the aura as changes in color. The effect of illness is to make the aura duller or to mark it with patches of new color.

"When a healer places his hands upon a patient," Turner explains, "there is an immediate blending together of their auras. Within a few minutes all other colors that were previously observable become subordinated by a prevailing blue, which extends greatly beyond normal and seems to fill the room in which treatment is being carried out. . . . It is still possible to see the colors that had denoted symptoms, but these float away from the body of the patient and become surrounded by a yellow colored light which seems to be spinning. What follows is for all the world like the action of a 'spiritual penicillin.' The yellow light gradually overcomes the duller color of the disease and it becomes flattened out and much less intense."

Many patients have spoken of the feelings of energy and warmth that pass into them during the moments of healing. Turner describes an interesting experiment in which unexposed film was placed between the healer's hands and the patient in a darkened room. When the film was developed, markings were discovered on it similar to those that can be made by holding film close to an electric stove in a darkened kitchen. A control experiment was performed using someone who lacked the power to heal. No markings were visible.

Many healers now perform much of their work by the method known as "absent" healing. One way is to ask the patients who

Although Edwards does not claim to do "instant" cures, some of his results appear to be so.
Above: one patient suffering from spinal problems and arthritis approached the platform leaning heavily on his walking stick.

Right: after his treatment, he walked confidently around the platform, managed the steps without his stick, and walked easily back to his original seat. A month later he was not only walking, but also riding a bicycle.

cannot get to the healer to sit quietly each day at a certain time. At the same time the healer will slowly read out each patient's name asking that healing may be given. He might then make a general request for healing for all the other people on his absent healing list whose conditions are less severe. After a period of meditation the intercession, or appeal by the healer on behalf of the sick, is over.

Distance between healer and patient appears to have no adverse effect on treatment. The healer projects his thoughts both toward the sick person and toward the spiritual world, and once the link has been established the healing forces flow where they are directed. Turner contrasts the success of this method with the relatively poor results obtained when people pray directly for themselves. It is as though the healing process requires someone else to appeal on a person's behalf.

In 1944 Harry Edwards' house was wrecked by a German bomb, and his record book and healing register destroyed. "In losing that register," he says, "it was as if the very bottom had fallen out of life itself, for I knew that absent healing work had received a very heavy blow. All I could then do was to recall from my memory as many cases as I could for directive intercession for the remainder."

He expected a marked falling off in the good progress his patients were reporting, but to his astonishment he found that the percentage of improvements was actually increasing. This caused him to review his manner of work, and from that period on he stopped making timed absent healing appointments except in emergency cases. The explanation for the unexpectedly good reports may be that his quality as a receiving and transmitting agent for the healing powers had reached such a high degree of development that he could become an open channel. All that he does today is to make a mental note of the names of the patients as he reads their letters requesting treatment. The

Below: one well-known spiritual healer, Gordon Turner, turned his gifts to the animal kingdom as well. Although in his career he treated many animals—ranging from bears and elephants to the more ordinary domestic pets—he was not ever bitten or scratched.

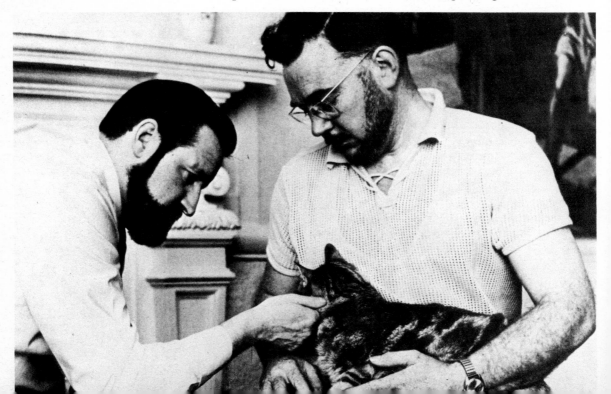

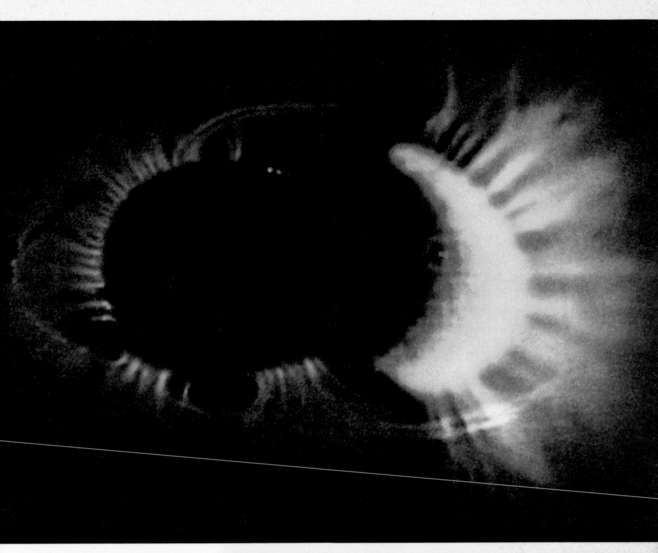

One of the most persistent claims of Spiritualism is that mediums can discern an aura, or field of color, around the human body. A Russian electrical mechanic, Semyon Kirlian, developed a kind of photography that produced an image of an aura surrounding living matter—a brilliantly colored pattern of flares and rays with lightninglike effects. Above: the finger pad of a faith healer, photographed by the Kirlian method at the very moment when she was treating a patient. Right: the faith healer's finger pad at rest, before she began her treatment. Healers have often spoken of the energy they generate going out to correct an improper energy balance in their patients. Is this photographic proof of that interpretation of their work?

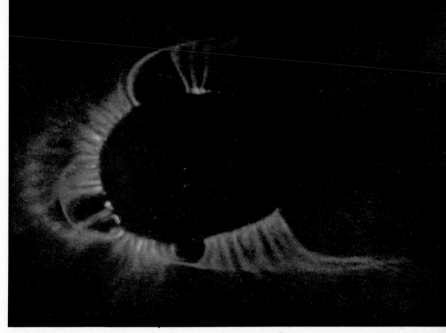

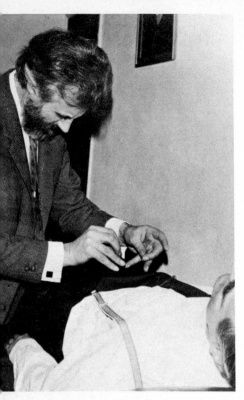

Above: medium George Chapman in trance. There are witnesses who say that the former well-known doctor, William Lang, operates on patients through Chapman's mediumship. Those who knew Dr. Lang in life claim that his voice and mannerisms are taken on by Chapman during these trance operations, though Chapman had never met the doctor.

Below: Dr. William Lang. He was an eminent eye specialist and a particularly skilled surgeon.

healing force then flows directly to them by this simple act.

Healers like Edwards and Turner are *directed* by their spirit guides. Another type of healer will enter a trance and while in that state be *controlled* by a spirit. One of the most interesting of these is George Chapman, an ex-fireman from Liverpool, England. He turned to Spiritualism after the death of his baby daughter in 1945. The messages he received proved to his satisfaction that life continued after death, and also led him to become a medium. In his trance state he received messages from a spiritual healing band that included "Lone Star," a member of the Cree tribe of Indians, and a Chinese surgeon named Chang. But these slipped into the background after the spirit of Dr. William Lang presented itself.

The association between Chapman and Dr. Lang is one of the most enigmatic in spirit healing. Lang was born in 1852. He became an eminent eye doctor, and published several works concerning diseases of the eye. He died in 1937 at the age of 84. Chapman was then a boy of 16. Ten years later Lang's voice began speaking through Chapman's mouth, and he was eventually able to assume complete control of Chapman while he was in trance.

When this occurs Chapman's face becomes wrinkled, his body hunches slightly, and he speaks in an "elderly, old-fashioned" voice that Lang's old associates have recognized as the voice of their former colleague. If Lang thinks an operation is necessary Chapman, controlled by Lang, moves his fingers over the body of the patient who remains conscious and fully clothed. He uses invisible spirit surgical instruments to perform an invisible operation on the spirit body.

Chapman believes the spirit body he and Dr. Lang operate on to be composed of electric cells supplying energy to the physical body. When illness develops in the physical body a corresponding change occurs in the spirit body. In the same way an operation performed on the spirit body can alter the condition of the physical body.

Once Chapman is in trance his own spirit self is temporarily withdrawn from his body, and Dr. Lang takes over. Mrs. Kathleen Vaughan, transport officer of the Red Cross Ambulance Service in Croydon, London, described Chapman's state when he does a trance healing. She drove a patient the 40 miles to see Chapman in Aylesbury, Buckinghamshire, and then stayed to watch. Here is what she says in *Extraordinary Encounters* (1973), collected by George Chapman.

"His eyes were closed," she reports, "and during the whole time we were with him they never moved, whereas in sleep there is usually some movement of the eyeball . . . He asked the patient how he could help her and she gave a very simple description of her immediate failing. He examined her sitting upright in a chair less than an arm's length away from me. He diagnosed a trapped artery to the spine and said he would operate.

"I helped her onto the couch and straightened her clothing. He told her to close her eyes and breathe deeply, and then he said, 'Come on, Basil,' snapped his fingers, and appeared to be handed what he needed for the operation. I stood right behind him, watching every movement. He said to me, 'I must operate on the heart, but don't worry, fortunately it is very strong.' He then started to operate in silence, except for the snap of his fingers indicating the instrument he required. All this took place about an inch above the patient's body. I was amazed at the precision and skill of the whole thing. Then he told me he would try to change the chemical action of the fluid to the spine. We brought the patient back to the chair, so that I could see all that was going on, and Dr. Lang gave her an injection on every vertebra right up to the brain.

"I had seen Dr. Lang make about 60 stitches after operating, but without touching the patient. When I told her this she could not believe it. She said she felt every move that was made. The stitching was very apparent to her, though not painfully so, as she had felt the flesh drawing together."

Several patients have commented on Dr. Lang's habit of snapping and clicking his fingers. Madame Siri Biro, the distinguished concert pianist, was treated by Chapman for an illness brought on by her allergy to penicillin. She says, "Dr. Lang explained to me that he has invisible helpers who know, by the way he clicks his fingers, which instrument he requires."

Lang's son Basil is one of these helpers, and in conversation with Dr. Robert W. Laidlaw, member of the American Society for Psychical Research, Lang explained that his son is being trained in the spirit world to take over from him. After George Chapman dies, the healing association will be continued between Basil Lang and Chapman's son Michael.

A determined materialist finds such phenomena hard to credit. Yet healing acts considerably more bizarre are performed daily as a matter of course in Brazil and in the Philippines. The psychic operations performed by the late José Arigó, Edivaldo Silva, and Lourival de Freitas in Brazil, and by Antonio Agpaoa, Mercardo, and their compatriots in the Philippines, have been the subject of much speculation in recent years. Accusations of trickery abound. People who have not witnessed psychic surgery maintain it is impossible for an invisible scalpel to produce visible spurts of blood, and that an abdomen roughly opened for an operation cannot heal in an instant and leave the skin unscarred. The feats of José Pedro de Freitas, better known as José Arigó, cannot have taken place, skeptics say. Yet the evidence mounts up to suggest they positively did.

Arigó's first psychic operation was reported in 1956 by a Brazilian senator who said Arigó had successfully removed a tumor from his colon with a knife and no anesthesia. Arigó himself said he did not remember this incident, but he willingly acknowledged what happened two months later. On this occasion he cut open a dying woman with a butcher knife and removed a uterine tumor weighing 14 pounds. The woman survived and was still alive 12 years later.

Inquiries into Arigó's background revealed that this good-natured clerk and former tin miner had become increasingly subject to fainting fits. Night after night he would enter a trance state during which, so he told his alarmed wife, a bald, fat-bellied man would appear before him and say in a German accent, "You will cure many." Arigó, a dutiful Catholic, had

The Surgeon who Operates on the Spirit Body

Dr. William Lang died in 1937, but he is practicing today in a town just north of London—or so say many who have consulted him. Patients who come to see him meet him in a curtained room. He talks to them, diagnoses the complaint, and then, if necessary, operates on them. Because Dr. Lang operates on the spirit body, the patient remains fully clothed. His hands move swiftly and surely, although his eyes are closed, to correct the difficulty in the patient's spirit body—and such correction enables the physical body to function properly.

Patients may have met the medium George Chapman before he went into the trance that allows Dr. Lang to appear, but they report that he is quite unlike the formerly well-known surgeon. Dr. Lang's voice is a little quavery and high-pitched, and his shoulders are stooped. Those who knew him in life say it is unmistakably Dr. Lang.

Patients report that they can feel Dr. Lang at work. During the operation his warm friendly manner sometimes grows sharp, and he snaps his fingers peremptorily to indicate which instruments he wants passed by his spirit assistants. Patients say they feel safe in Dr. Lang's hands—though the hands are unseen.

called in the priest to exorcise the devil, but as the pressure to become a healing medium grew stronger he left the Catholic religion and became a Spiritist, the name for Spiritualist in France and South America. The man with the German accent proved to be his spirit control Dr. Adolf Fritz, a Munich-born doctor thought to have died in Estonia in 1918.

Arigó had become a national hero by the time of his death in a car accident in 1971. Hundreds of thousands of Brazilians had made the journey to the picturesque hillside town of Congonhas to be treated by him. He would work throughout the morning and from late afternoon until far into the evening examining the crowds of patients, rich and poor, who besieged the tumbledown building he used as his healing center. Working in full view of anybody who cared to stand near him, he would write out a prescription or perform an operation at incredible speed, sometimes taking less than one minute between making the incision and closing it again.

These operations took place without any anesthetic or any kind of sterilization, but in most cases there seems to have been no pain—at most "a slight tickling"—nor did anyone suffer blood poisoning. Dr. Ary Lex, a Sao Paolo surgeon and lecturer, witnessed several operations and even held the arm of one patient while Arigó removed a nonmalignant tumor from it. In this case Arigó did not cut the skin. "He sort of rubbed the skin with the back of his scapel," Lex explained. "He then squeezed the lipoma [tumor] with his fingers and it came out whole."

Dr. Anrija Puharich, the New York neurologist who studied and filmed Arigó at work in 1968, witnessed one of his most unnerving surgical feats—an eye operation for which his only instrument would be a pair of nail scissors or a penknife. Puharich was asked to take hold of the penknife Arigó had left stuck under the eyebrow. He said: "Although the blade was dug deep into the man's eye there appeared to be no fluidity of tissue in the interior, almost as if the blade were driving between the cells."

Even more puzzling than this rough treatment is the phenomenon of instant healing, vouched for by all who have seen or experienced psychic surgery. After completing an operation Arigó simply pressed the two pieces of flesh together and they stayed together, leaving only a thin red line that soon faded. Guy Playfair, an English writer who lived in Brazil for many years, gives an account of his own operation in his book *The Flying Cow*, published in 1975. His healer was Edivaldo Silva, known generally simply as Edivaldo, a schoolteacher whose spirit controls include doctors from several countries as well as Arigó's Dr. Fritz. The operation took place in Rio de Janeiro in another ramshackle building—for though psychic surgery is tolerated by the law it is still illegal. Playfair was aware of Edivaldo's thumbs penetrating his abdominal wall, but felt no pain. When he looked at his stomach afterward the only sign of the operation was a thin jagged line about three inches long, which disappeared overnight, and two bright red dots that have never faded.

Like the other healing mediums Edivaldo works in a trance

Above: the late famous Brazilian psychic surgeon José Arigó, being questioned during his trial in 1964. He was imprisoned for practicing medicine illegally. He served less than half of his sentence, and returned home to scenes of wild celebration by his numerous jubilant supporters.

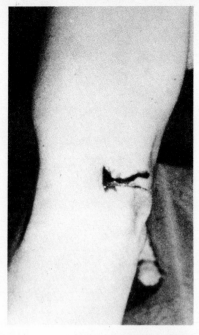

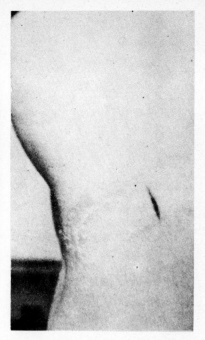

Above: psychic researcher Dr. Andrija Puharich went to study Arigó and ended up being operated on for a lipoma in his arm. These pictures show the wound just after surgery (left) and only two days later, almost entirely healed.

Above: the knife Arigó used for the surgery, and the lipoma that was excised from Puharich's arm.

Left: a magazine article about Puharich's operation. Besides using his own experience as evidence, Puharich and his team followed up several hundred cases, and reported that Arigó's success rate was about 95 percent.

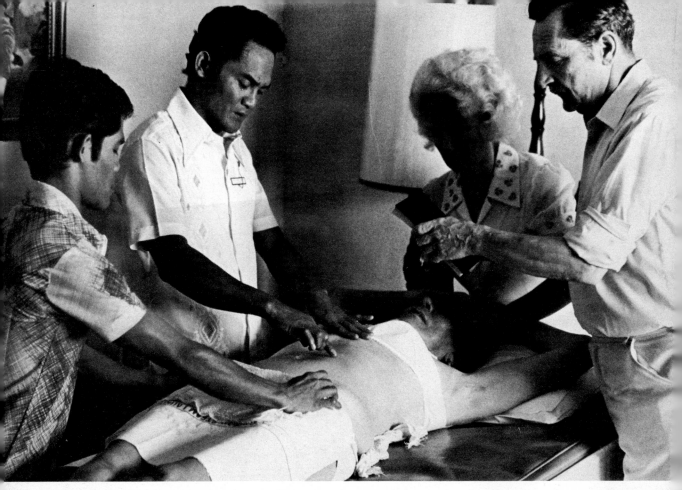

state, and has no idea why his treatments work. Playfair came across so much paranormal activity in Brazil—"the world's most psychic country"—that he felt he had to find the explanation. He does not exclude the possibility of occasional fraud, although he feels that healers only fall back on this when, as must sometimes happen, the spirit fails them. Despite the extraordinary nature of their achievements, neither Arigó nor Edivaldo has ever been accused of trickery—unlike the psychic healers of the Philippines who have not borne up so well under investigation.

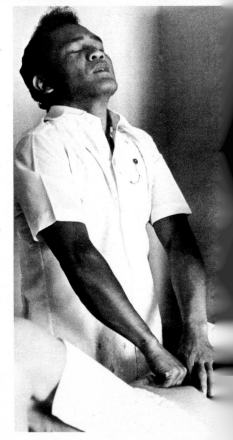

Harold Sherman, the veteran ESP researcher from Arkansas, closely studied the working methods of Antonio Agpaoa in Manila and, since he seems to have liked Agpaoa personally, regretfully recorded the evidence against his wonder cures. More recently, a British television team examined the work of another Filipino healer who appeared to remove bleeding pieces of tissue from gaping incisions that left no scar. These wonders were shown to be the work of a skilled illusionist. Two doctors, one an amateur conjuror, posed as patients and recognized the tricks.

It is possible that some of these tricks are window dressing, intended to make a patient feel he has undergone an operation even though his illness has been treated by other means, perhaps by suggestion. This possibility is considered by Dr. Lyall Watson who describes Filipino psychic healing in his book *The Romeo Error*, published in 1974. In this connection it is interesting that Edivaldo should have told Guy Playfair the

Filipino psychic surgeons at work, as filmed for British television. Left: the surgeon marks the spot to make his incision. One of the onlookers shades the patient's eyes. Below left: the surgeon appears to thrust his fingers into the patient's abdomen, having made an incision with his bare hands. (Skeptics point out that it is easy—given the average flabby abdomen—to fake the effect of fingers disappearing into a body.) Below: withdrawing a "growth."

spirits were already treating his patients while they waited in the queue to see him.

Theories that rely on suggestion and hypnotism, however, leave too much unexplained. Playfair suggests that there may be a preexistent biological model for all living structures, located outside our physical world but connected to it possibly through the brain. Since this model would not represent diseased or damaged tissue, any person who obtained access to it might possess the means to recreate living tissue. Research is continuing in Brazil and has recently been taken up in Czechoslovakia and the Soviet Union. Until the outcome of such research is known, the principles governing the work of the Brazilian Spiritists must remain tantalizingly unexplained.

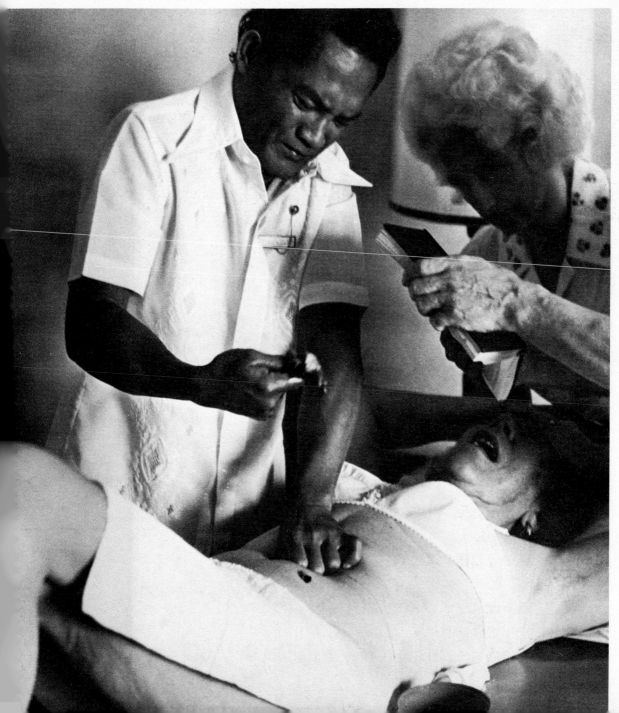

6

The Triumph of Hypnotism

Paris in the years leading up to the French Revolution was a hotbed of scientific marvels. Benjamin Franklin, the American ambassador, had started a craze for demonstrations of electricity. A chess-playing robot drew crowds of intrigued onlookers. In 1783 humans had risen from the ground for the first time in history, and had gone floating across the countryside in a balloon. As a source of argument, enthusiasm, and scandal, however, nothing equalled the healing seances of Dr. Franz Anton Mesmer.

The medical fraternity of Paris detested this foreigner from Vienna with his new-fangled theory of "animal magnetism." But

The extraordinary power of the hypnotist over a receptive subject has fascinated the general public and writers of fact and fiction since hypnotism was developed in the wake of Franz Mesmer's work. Since then hypnotism has had a checkered career, but is once again coming to be considered less a theatrical stunt than a legitimate technique for healing. Right: a 19th-century German view of a hypnotist and his subject.

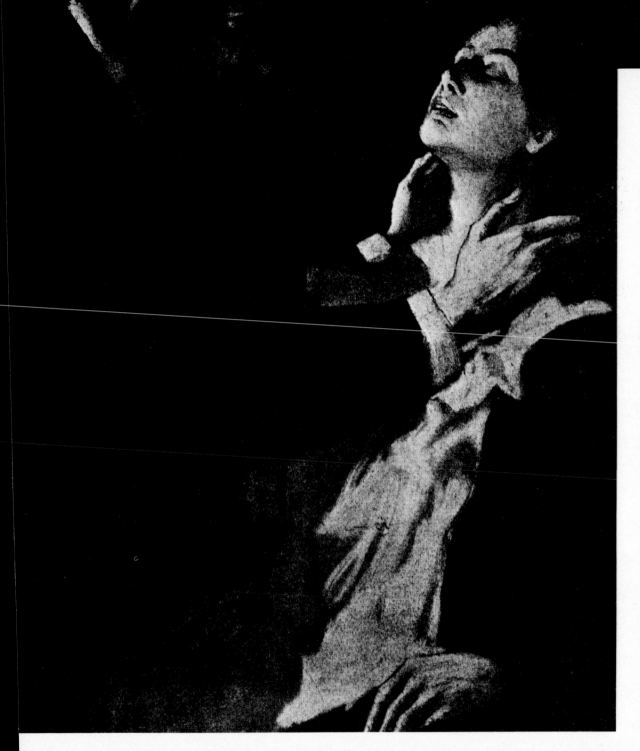

"Patients cried out hysterically or fainted with excitement"

Below: Franz Anton Mesmer shown treating an invalid by magnetic contact. His theory was that the Universe was filled with a magnetic fluid. Illness was a result of imbalance in this fluid, and magnetic contact could restore the proper flow.

Parisians of all classes flocked to the salon of their latest miracle-healer. The room in which they assembled was richly furnished and hung with mirrors. Thick carpets covered the floor; drawn curtains shut out the world. The company sat close together around a piece of apparatus known as the *baguet*, an oak tub containing water and iron filings, and a number of flasks filled with so-called magnetized water. From the baguet protruded a number of iron rods and cords which the patients held against the affected parts of their bodies. In the background soft music was played on wind instruments or on Mesmer's celebrated glass harmonica. Gradually the music quickened, and patients cried out hysterically or fainted with excitement.

At the height of the session Mesmer himself entered, a commanding figure in a robe of purple silk trimmed with lace. He moved from patient to patient, fixing them with his penetrating gaze or touching them with his elegant iron wand. Women patients collapsed and were borne off by attendants to the mattress-lined crisis room. Others went into trance. When they recovered their senses, many of them were cured.

The majority of them had nervous afflictions, though none of the symptoms were the less genuine for that. Contemporary accounts speak of cures for migraine, asthma, paralysis, blindness, deafness, and a wide variety of internal disorders. One who wrote an account of his cure was the Chevalier de Haussay, an infantry major. He had suffered years of ill-health brought on by an attack of frostbite in Hanover, followed by malignant fever contracted in Martinique. When he came to see

Above: an anti-Mesmer cartoon
—of which there were many—
shows Mesmer's salon as a
scene of lascivious activities.

Right: Mesmer, the inventor of
animal magnetism, as depicted
by another unkind caricaturist.
Mesmer himself was completely
sincere, as oblivious as his
critics of the mechanism of his
cures. For him, all the trap-
pings were an essential part of
his treatment of the suffering.

Mesmer he staggered, spoke with difficulty, laughed for no
reason, and suffered from constant tremors. His eyes also
started from their sockets. Mesmer's treatment produced a
series of shuddering fits—"ice coming from my limbs, followed
by great heat and foetid perspiration," as he put it. "Now after
four months," the statement ends, "I am completely cured."

Mesmer, who was a sincere and honest man, believed he
worked these cures by communicating a form of healing magnetism to his patients. In his day magnetism was still a baffling
phenomenon, just as were electricity and many other wonders
we now take for granted. But some scientists were beginning to
think of it in terms of a universal force. In his doctoral thesis
written in Vienna 20 years before, Mesmer had argued that the
stars might influence human beings by means of a magnetic fluid
that filled the universe. If the constant flow of this fluid in the
body was disturbed, illness would result. Health could be
restored by reestablishing the flow.

In his early days in Vienna Mesmer stroked his sick patients
with magnets, but gradually he discovered he could do away
with these aids. For a while he touched people with his own
hands. Finally he found that staring intently into their eyes was
enough to establish what he called a *rapport*. He concluded that
certain people like himself were able to concentrate the universal magnetic fluid and cause it to flow to others. Objects too
could be magnetized—clothes, trees, even his glass harmonica.
He called this power "animal magnetism."

In 1784 Louis XVI set up a commission to examine Mesmer's

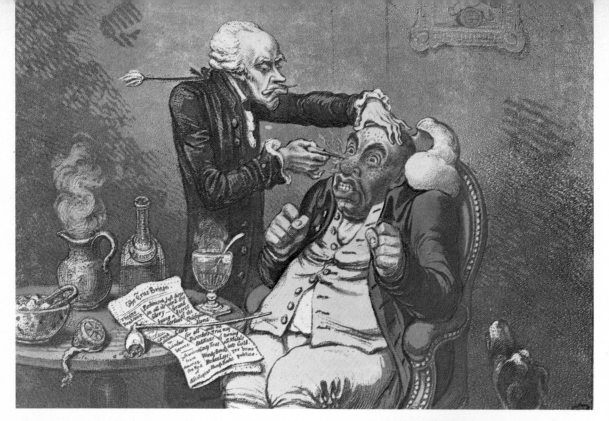

Above: the mysterious effects of magnetism were exploited as a curative agent in another bizarre direction by Elisha Perkins' "metallic tractors," patented in 1798. These peculiar rods were supposed to draw out disease at its source. It became sufficiently popular as a treatment to provoke cartoon hilarity, as shown here.

Right: the Marquis de Puységur, one of Mesmer's enthusiastic followers, set about curing people by mesmerizing a tree to serve as a focus for treatment. This contemporary but inaccurate drawing shows him not only mesmerizing the tree, but everyone in the general vicinity as well.

claims. Its members included Benjamin Franklin, then Ambassador to France, and a certain Dr. Joseph Guillotin, later to earn immortality as the inventor of "a painless beheading machine." The commission investigated Mesmer's magnetic tubs, and drank glasses of his magnetized water. The verdict was that they were useless—a not surprising conclusion since they failed to take into account the one essential part of the treatment, the presence of Dr. Mesmer himself.

Neither Mesmer nor his critics ever grasped the true significance of his system. The commission reported disdainfully "that imagination played a part in the effects produced by animal magnetism." They did not consider what influenced the imagination—or how it did so—although a confidential report accompanying the official findings hinted darkly at "feelings of sexual attachment."

One member of the commission, Jean Sylvain Bailly, later mayor of Paris, did comment on the different reactions of individual patients to magnetism. He was surprised by "the excessive agitation of some and the profound tranquillity of others." This was all the more curious because "all of the patients were under the domination of the same magnetizer." Bailly, like Mesmer, thought of the force as something that could pass, presumably in equal quantities, from one person to another. They did not see that mesmerism, as it was coming to be called, was an intangible power of the mind.

Mesmer lived until 1815, and continued to believe in his magnetic fluid. The implications of his work were developed by others.

Two French aristocrats were the first to observe that a mesmerized patient obeyed the instructions of his mesmerist. The Marquis de Puysegur and his brother Count Maxime had become enthusiastic mesmerists in Paris. When they returned to their chateau in Buzancy near Soissons they set about curing the local peasants. They magnetized a large elm tree on the village green and hung cords from the branches. "Below this mysterious tree," wrote an eye witness, "several circular stone benches have been erected. The sick sit on them and tie the cord round the parts of their bodies which are diseased. Then the session begins. The patients touch each other's thumbs, and thus the magnetic fluid circulates freely . . ."

In these natural surroundings there were none of the frenzied crises that had been seen in Mesmer's salon. There was, however, one development the Puysegur brothers had not anticipated. A peasant of 23, Victor Race, came to be treated for an inflammation of the lungs. "What was my surprise," the Marquis later wrote, "to see, at the end of a few minutes this man fall asleep in my arms, quite limp, with no signs of pain or any convulsions. I continued the magnetizing, he trembled and started to talk aloud about his troubles. As he seemed distressed I stopped him and tried to inspire him with more cheerful things. This was very easy to do, and soon he showed every sign of cheerfulness, hopping on his chair and miming a song, which I made him repeat out loud. The next day he could not remember my visit of the previous evening but he said he never felt better."

The Magnetized Tree that Cured

Many French aristocrats of the 18th century cared little about the peasants living near their grand chateaux. But the Marquis de Puységur and his brother Count Maxime did. After becoming enthusiastic followers of Dr. Franz Mesmer in Paris, they returned to their country estate to apply Mesmer's method of healing to all the local inhabitants. This involved using magnetism to harness the powers of the magnetic fluid present in the Universe, which Mesmer said existed and could cure disease and illness.

The two brothers magnetized the large elm tree in the center of the village near their country home, and hung down long cords that dangled from the branches. Sufferers sat under the tree on circular stone benches, and tied the cords around the parts of the body in which they felt pain. Then they touched each other's thumbs to allow the magnetic fluid to flow from one to the other and at the same time to circulate freely among them.

In the humble village square there was none of the elegance of Mesmer's rooms. No soothing music. No finely dressed ladies and gentlemen. But curiously enough, people who sat under the magnetized elm tree got well—just as many did in the Paris salon.

Left: the Abbé Faria hypnotizing his patients by look and command alone. By his time, all the paraphernalia of Mesmer's time—the magnets, the magnetic fluids, and so forth—had been found unnecessary to achieve results.

Right: a caricature of about 1816 labeling the Abbé Faria as the Great Charlatan, and mocking his hypnotic grip on people.

The Marquis mesmerized Victor again. Normally a slow speaker, he talked freely and intelligently while in trance. He also stood up and walked about in obedience to his master's orders. Evidently, thought Puysegur, the way Mesmer's magnetic fluid operated must be through a person's mind, by the power of suggestion.

Victor showed one other remarkable ability. When mesmerized he could diagnose the diseases of his fellow-sufferers around the tree, and suggest the proper treatment. Soon other mesmerist circles in France were demonstrating similar clairvoyant powers. In the aftermath of the French Revolution the next generation of mesmerists traveled through England and America, where their shows and cures became a popular wonder. A pupil of Puysegur taught Phineas P. Quimby who in turn taught Mary Baker Eddy, the founder of Christian Science. Other American mesmerists, notably Andrew Jackson Davis, known as the "Poughkeepsie Seer," applied their clairvoyant talents to Spiritualism and Theosophy.

In the 1820s a Portuguese abbot, the Abbe Faria, came to the conclusion that magnetic fluids, if they existed at all, played no part in the cures. In his healing practice in Paris, where he made extensive use of mesmerism, he realized that the factor essential to success was a receptive attitude in the patient.

This was helpful up to a point. It did away with the iron rods, the cords, the magnetized trees. But science was still no closer to finding what caused a patient to be receptive to the suggestions of his mesmerist. The Abbe had merely to tell his patients to go to sleep, and immediately they fell asleep.

Another puzzling phenomenon discovered about this time

was what is now called post-hypnotic suggestion. This occurs when a hypnotized person is instructed to perform a certain task at a particular time or on receipt of a particular signal, even though by that time he has awakened from his trance. For example, a subject is told that he will bend down and take off his shoes when the mesmerist blows his nose twice. On being wakened from his trance he has no memory of the instruction. Half an hour later the mesmerist blows his nose twice. At once the subject becomes uneasy. He shifts his feet, he stares at the floor. Finally, unable to bear some inner tension any longer, he bends down and removes his shoes. Sometimes he will go to ingenious lengths to account for his strange action, such as explaining that he feels an itch in both his big toes.

The mesmerist—or hypnotist as he later came to be called—can also alter a subject's powers of perception. A person in a hypnotic trance, given a book to hold and then told there is nothing in his hand, will neither see it nor feel it. For some reason still unknown his full consciousness is shut off from it. His mind will also accept misleading information. To give the popular fairground example: the hypnotized subject will chew his way through a raw potato with every sign of enjoyment if he is told it is a ripe apple.

Other parts of the body's nervous system are also affected by hypnotic suggestion. A subject is told he is going to be touched with a red-hot wire. When a cold wire is placed against his skin he cries out in pain. More interesting still, a blister forms where his skin was touched. On the other hand, if he is touched with a red-hot wire but told it is cold, he will feel no pain and no blister will form.

Above: Dr. James Braid, a Scot who introduced the new term "hypnotism." It afterward supplanted mesmerism as a description of the sleeplike trance of patients being treated.

Above: medical hypnosis in the 19th century. The woman patient has been told that there is a snake about to strike her (as indicated by the dotted line), and she believes she sees it. Below: Dr. Ambroise-Auguste Liébeault in his clinic in Nancy, France about 1900. For 20 years he worked practically unnoticed, but when outside investigators came to him they were favorably impressed by his therapeutic work.

This interruption of normal sensory perception was the next feature of mesmerism to be developed. Unfortunately for the protagonists it occurred in England, where the majority of the medical practitioners were even more suspicious of unorthodox ideas than their French colleagues.

John Elliotson was the first Englishman to make use of a stethoscope, for example, and was abused for this. "Do you use that hocus pocus?" a senior physician snapped at him. "You will learn nothing by it, and if you do, you cannot treat disease the better."

Elliotson was virtually the founder of London's University College Hospital, the first hospital to be coordinated with a medical college so as to give students the opportunity for clinical research. After witnessing a French demonstration of mesmerism in 1837 he immediately realized that here at last was an answer to the eternal problem of surgical pain. He began mesmerizing his own patients, and amputations of the thigh, leg, arm, and breast were painlessly performed during mesmeric trance. Former colleagues who witnessed these operations stubbornly asserted that the patients must have been trained not to express pain.

In addition to its anesthetic value mesmerism was especially helpful in treating hysteria and other functional nervous disorders. Mesmer himself had declared that his system "could help only people suffering from nervous disorders and no others." Like Mesmer, Elliotson was accused of encouraging immorality. Mesmerism, Dr. Francis Hawkins declared before an audience of doctors, "is the especial favorite of those, both male and female, in whom the sexual passions burn strongly, either in secret or notoriously. Decency forbids me to be more explicit."

The dignified reply given by Elliotson was as follows: "Mesmeric attraction has nothing sexual in it; it is of the

purest kind, simple friendship, and indeed exactly like the love of a young child for its mother, for it seems characterized by a feeling of safety when with the mesmerist, and of fear of others."

The Scottish surgeon John Esdaile was marginally more fortunate than Elliotson in that he performed his first mesmeric experiments in India while attached to the Native Hospital in Hooghly. His successes with amputations were so impressive that in 1846 the government of Bengal put him in charge of a small hospital in Calcutta, renamed the Mesmeric Hospital. Before he retired from India five years later he had performed thousands of painless minor operations for the removal of large scrotal tumors. This was a condition not uncommon in India at that time, but the removal of them was considered so dangerous that few surgeons attempted it. One of the tumors removed by Esdaile weighed 103 pounds, and was as heavy as the patient's body. To perform the operation the tumor had to be supported by means of a rope and pulley in the rafters.

Esdaile still believed that mesmerism worked because a healing fluid was capable of being poured from one person to another. It was his contemporary James Braid—another Scotsman—who removed the last of the mysticism from animal magnetism. He realized that the mesmeric trance was a purely subjective phenomenon. "The subject is not put to sleep; he goes to sleep." He introduced the new term—*Neurohypnotism*, or nervous sleep, which he described as "a peculiar condition of the nervous system produced by artificial contrivance." For the sake of brevity the name was shortened to the one we use today: hypnotism. It comes from the Greek word *hypnos*, meaning sleep.

The concept of the unconscious did not exist in Braid's day, but he managed to demonstrate what he called the "dual consciousness" of the mind. While his patients were under hypnosis he taught them fragments of foreign languages. They forgot these foreign words when they were awake, but remembered them again the next time they were hypnotized.

Esdaile and Braid were unlucky in that ether and chloroform were introduced at just this time. Doctors took readily to these physical agents of anesthesia as something whose action they could understand. Hypnotism, which they could not or refused to understand, could be safely ignored. If Braid had not prepared a paper on his work and sent it to a colleague in Paris shortly before his death in 1860, his work would have died with him. As it was, it lay dormant in England for 30 years.

Braid's Parisian colleague read his paper to the French Academy in 1860. In the audience there happened to be a quiet hard-working country doctor destined to be the pioneer of hypnotherapy. He was Ambroise-Auguste Liébeault. After listening attentively to Braid's theories he returned to his hometown of Nancy where he added hypnotism to his treatment of the local peasants. He was a man the peasants trusted, and he knew how to persuade them to cooperate with him. "If you wish me to treat you with drugs," he said to them, "I will do so, but you will have to pay me as before. However, if you will allow me to hypnotize you, I will do it for nothing."

Above: Professor Hippolyte Bernheim. He went to Nancy to debunk Liébeault after he heard that Liébeault had cured a patient whom he himself had treated without success. But he was convinced of Liébeault's method when he understood it, and often practiced it himself.

An eye witness reports that his clinic, invariably thronged, consisted of two rooms in a corner of his garden. He would settle the patient in a comfortable armchair, ask him to close his eyes, and then suggest to him that he was falling asleep. "Your eyelids are getting heavy, your limbs feel numb, you are becoming more and more drowsy . . ." This method of inducing hypnotism is essentially the one still practiced today. Liébeault was aware, as Mesmer had not been, that the trance had no healing value in itself, but was simply a means to help the patient to concentrate on what he was told. When his patients were hypnotized he found he could suggest away many of their nervous disorders.

It is possible to see in "the good father" Liébeault the first representative of a new kind of doctor—unassuming, undogmatic, trying and persisting with a new method because it seemed to work even though the reason it worked was not understood. Liébeault wrote a book about his cases in 1866, and it is said that only one copy was sold. It was nearly 20 years before his work became generally known outside Nancy. He was discovered in 1882 by Hippolyte Bernheim, a doctor with a national reputation who heard that Liébeault had cured a case of sciatica on which Bernheim himself had worked in vain for six months. Bernheim went to Nancy prepared to expose Liébeault as a charlatan, watched him at work—and immediately became his pupil.

Many years later Sigmund Freud recorded the visit he paid to Nancy as a young man. He wrote: "I witnessed the moving spectacle of old Liébeault working among the poor women and children of the laboring classes, I was a spectator of Bernheim's astonishing experiments upon his hospital patients, and I received the profoundest impression of the possibility that there could be powerful mental processes which nevertheless remained hidden from the consciousness of man."

Freud had come to France on a traveling fellowship to study under the great neurologist Jean Martin Charcot. Unlike Liébeault and Bernheim, who sought to cure the sick, Charcot's interest lay in demonstrating phenomena—in particular, hysterical phenomena. Ideas about hysteria had been confused for centuries. Most people thought it a condition suffered chiefly if not solely by women, and for a long time it was said to be caused when the uterus became detached and wandered to another part of the body. The name hysteria in fact comes from the Greek word *hystera*, womb. The removal of an ovary to cure hysteria was the prescribed treatment as late as 1882. In Charcot's view, hypnosis was an abnormal state associated with hysteria. He studied its physical and neurological effects on 12 hysterical patients, all of them women. His findings had interest, but were necessarily limited by not taking into account any mental effects. Charcot also brought back the magnet, and some of his students endeavored to achieve cures by placing patients back to back with hysterics and trying to transfer the maladies from one to the other through magnetic influence.

Tricks like this appalled Liébeault, who in the course of his long life treated not 12 but 12,000 patients. They also offended Bernheim, who maintained that with rare exceptions all men

Left: Sigmund Freud as a young man. A student of Jean Martin Charcot, he visited Nancy in 1899 to watch Liébeault at work. He was greatly struck by the impact of Liébeault's work, and that of Bernheim, in harnessing powerful mental processes that could be used as healing tools.

Below: one of Charcot's classes. Charcot's interest in hypnotism was not in using it as a method of healing, but in using it to demonstrate kinds of hysterical phenomena. He studied the effects of hypnotism on only 12 patients, all of them women.

and all women—hysterical, neurotic, and normal—were susceptible to suggestion. Bernheim went on to say that the waking mind was powerfully swayed by suggestion, which accounted for such delusions as the Indian rope trick. He also examined the causes of crime. "Suggestion, no matter where it comes from, imposes itself upon our brains and plays a role in almost all crimes," he said. This foreshadowed much of 20th-century thinking. "In truth," he declared, "we are all potentially or actually hallucinating people during the greater part of our lives."

Freud kept a photograph of Charcot above his desk as a tribute, but within a few years he had gone far beyond his teacher. After it dawned on him that the symptoms of his neurotic patients were related to "impressive but forgotten scenes in their lives," he decided to use hypnosis as a means to help them talk of these scenes. A century earlier the Marquis de Puysegur had heard the peasant Victor speak of his personal troubles while in a trance. Freud was to develop this feature of the hypnotic trance in order to lead patients back through the events of their lives until they could come in touch again with forgotten incidents or phantasies that still, though unconsciously, troubled their minds. Neurotic symptoms, he believed,

Below: Professor Charcot in 1881. He had become the most famous neurologist of his day, and his clinic in Paris was the leading center for neuroclinical research in the world—the obvious place for young Dr. Freud to attend to further his neurological studies.

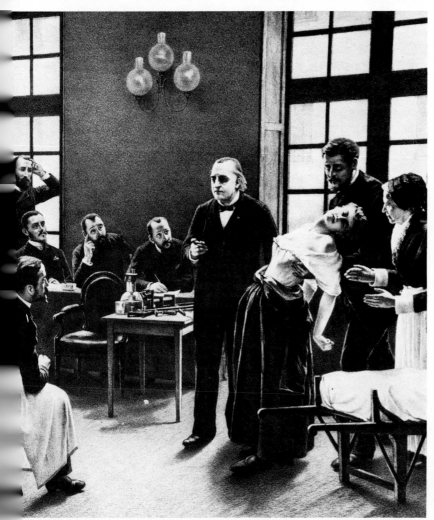

Left: Svengali hypnotizing the young and impressionable Trilby, in the novel by George du Maurier. Under his direction she became a brilliant singer, her talents disappearing abruptly when her manipulator collapsed and died.

Right and below: a modern-day Trilby who wants to dance in nightclubs is helped to shed her inhibitions by a hypnotist.

could thus be "talked away," although the forces that had caused the incidents to be forgotten, or repressed, inevitably made the process a lengthy one.

In time Freud was to discard hypnosis in favor of free association in which patients are encouraged to talk about whatever comes into their heads. Because one thought leads to another, it is hoped that sooner or later the repressed memories will be forced into the consciousness. The technique of free association marks the birth of psychoanalysis—but it was a birth in which hypnotism had acted as midwife.

Hypnotism now seemed to have come full circle from the Viennese Mesmer to the Viennese Freud in just over a hundred years. In popular imagination it had passed through many stages. Its emergence as a pervading element of fiction in the first half of the 19th century can be seen in the American writer Edgar Allen Poe. In his creepy short story "The Facts in the Case of M. Valdemar," the mind of the wretched Valdemar is kept alive within his dead and decomposing body by the power of mesmerism. Another common fear of hypnotism was expressed by the English writer George du Maurier in *Trilby*, published in 1894. In this book Svengali uses his mesmeric powers to turn a girl with a cracked voice into a superb opera singer. "He's mesmerized you," Trilby is warned ... "They get you into their power, and just to make you do any blessed thing they please— lie, murder, steal—anything! And kill yourself in the bargain when they've done with you."

A common belief today is that people cannot be hypnotized to do something they would normally refuse to do. This idea probably originates in an incident that occurred in Charcot's lecture room. Charcot was called away, leaving one of his

female subjects under hypnosis. A student, eager to try out his skill, suggested that she lift up her skirt. Instantly she snapped out of her trance, slapped him across the face, and walked out.

Recent research has tended to undermine this comforting view. The possibility of influencing a person's performance is illustrated by a case reported by Brian Inglis in his book *Fringe Medicine*, published in 1964. A golfer who found himself off his stride went to the British professional S. L. King for a lesson. He then went to a hypnotist who suggested to him that when he next played he would play exactly as King had showed him— except for four of the 18 holes. On these, the hypnotist suggested he would have to try to remember what King had told him, just as any golfer has to do after a lesson. The golfer went off, unaware of these instructions to his unconscious mind. His playing was superb for all but the designated four holes.

More ominous is the report of an experiment in which subjects were first shown the power of nitric acid to dissolve a coin, and then instructed to throw the beaker of acid—in fact, an identical beaker containing treated water—into the face of a laboratory assistant. Many threw the beaker. On one occasion the nitric acid was thrown when the hypnotist made what he calls "a most regrettable mistake in technique," and omitted to switch the beakers. Swift action prevented the formation of scars on the assistant's face. There is no record of the subject's reaction when he learned of the mishap.

Understanding of the hypnotic trance is still far from complete. It is known, however, to produce distinct physiological alterations, including changes of sugar content in the blood and of acid secretion in the stomach. Theories as to how it operates on the mind have scarcely advanced beyond the obvious

Right: for all its scientific
applications, hypnotism remains
a mysterious and fascinating
phenomenon to many people. So
there is still a place for the
stage hypnotist, as shown, to
excite and amaze an audience.

explanation that it isolates an area of the mental apparatus
from the rest of the brain.

Hypnosis is not likely to become a popular anesthetic in the
West even though it has none of the occasional dangers of drug-
based anesthesia. It shares with acupuncture the same disad-
vantage that Westerners do not like to see themselves being
operated on. In spite of this, hypnotic treatment has made some
headway in assisting painless childbirth. In the United States
too a number of dentists make use of it for teeth extraction.
Demonstrations have shown that when a patient is in a deep
trance, teeth can be extracted without pain and, even more
remarkable, without bleeding.

An astonishing cure that created a sensation among derma-
tologists occurred in England in the East Grinstead Hospital in
1951. It concerned a case of congenital ichthyosis, a condition
hitherto considered incurable, in which a black horny layer
spreads thickly over the skin. The patient was a boy of 16.
Warty excrescences covered his entire body except the chest,
neck, and face. This thick crust was perpetually cracking, with
resultant infection. He had been obliged to leave school because
the teachers and pupils objected to his smell. Skin from the
apparently normal chest had been grafted onto one hand, but
within a month had become indistinguishable from the rest of
the affected skin. Understandably shy and solitary, the boy saw
no hope in the future.

On February 10, 1951 he was hypnotized, and the suggestion
was made that the left arm would clear. About five days later

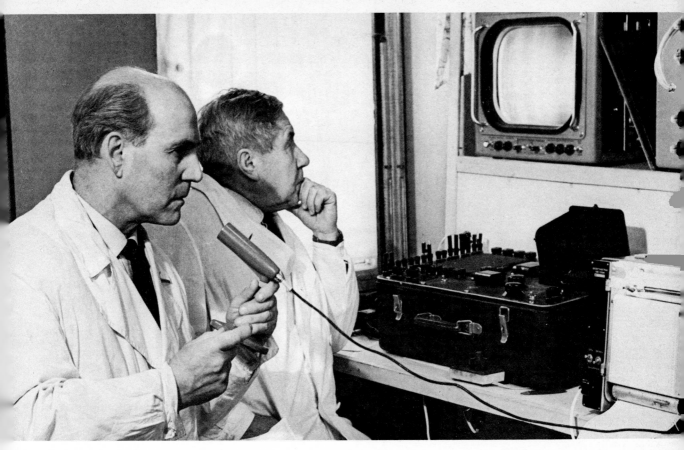

the horny layer softened and fell off. The skin underneath became pink and soft, and at the end of 10 days the arm was completely clear from shoulder to wrist. The right arm was treated in the same way, followed by the rest of the body. Some areas were only 70 per cent cleared, but the difference was enough to turn a lonely and despairing boy into someone described by his doctor as happy and normal. Eighteen months later he had a job as an electrician's assistant.

Dr. A. A. Mason, the doctor concerned, has stressed the extreme rarity of such a cure, and has subsequently made use of hypnosis chiefly as an adjunct to psychotherapy. This auxiliary role seems the most fruitful prospect for hypnosis. There is always a risk when hypnosis is used in isolation to treat a neurotic symptom, a physical manifestation, or even to cure addiction to smoking. The symptom may be removed, but not the underlying psychic cause of that symptom to which it may have served as the essential safety valve. Instances have been reported of patients who almost immediately succumb to a heart attack after being cured of chronic asthma by hypnosis. As long as the risks are recognized a skilled psychotherapist can use hypnosis to hasten the recall of traumatic memories, and to encourage reduction of the mind's resistance to self-knowledge. As an aid to psychotherapy the story of hypnotism is far from done. Mesmer was more prophetic than he knew when he headed his doctoral thesis with a verse by the Roman poet Horace: "Much will rise again that has long been buried, and much become submerged that is held in honor today."

Above: a Russian application of hypnosis has been to assist in therapy for patients suffering from bronchitis. They are placed in a special chamber with air at a very high pressure. The hypnosis is used to ease the discomfort the patients would normally feel in such a rarefied atmosphere—they are simply put into a deep hypnotic sleep. Below: the patients are kept under constant observation by means of a television screen.

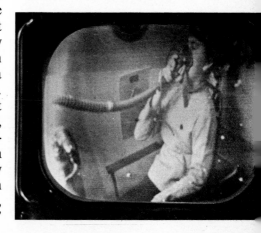

7

Mysterious Rays

It was probably as far back as 2000 B.C. that certain people found they had the power to locate underground water by dowsing. They would traverse an area holding a forked twig in their hands, and if they passed over water, seemingly involuntary movements in their muscles would cause the rod to move in a certain way. This indicated the presence of water. Later this skill was adapted to prospecting for minerals. In our own day it is also used to discover the location of buried pipes and cables on building sites, to trace missing persons, and to diagnose illness. Dowsers nowadays use a variety of instruments. Some use the traditional forked hazel twig, some a

From earliest times humans have felt that the Universe around them pulsed with mysterious powers beyond their understanding. The struggle to harness such power led to frequent failure, hot controversy, and perhaps from time to time, a degree of success. Right: one of the most disputed uses of mysterious rays is the energy accumulator or orgone box developed by Dr. Wilhelm Reich.

"Some sixth sense or faculty outside the normal human range"

Below: a dowser, from a book on dowsing published in 1733. His rod is clasped firmly in both hands, with his palms pointing upward. Dowsing seems to be a comparatively modern phenomenon. Although there are ancient myths of magical rods, there are no specific references in learned books to what we now know as dowsing until the Middle Ages.

whalebone rod. Others find that a small pendulum on a thread gives a more accurate response, while still others rely only on their bare hands. These last feel that it is the movement of the dowser's muscles that seems all-important, and the rods or pendulums are merely devices to help the dowser interpret such movements.

What actually causes the dowser's muscles to contract remains a mystery. Many dowsers believe that all substances give off different radiations which the human mind is capable of picking up, though it has to a large degree lost this ability as a result of relying on verbal communication. As Brian Inglis explains in his book *Fringe Medicine*: "Most people when discussing one of the phenomena of ESP, such as clairvoyance or telepathy, think of it (whether they believe in it or not) as a mental process, but diviners assume that it will eventually be accounted for by radiations. Every form of matter radiates on its own wavelength; the human mind, they believe, contains a built-in receiving station capable of tuning in to these broadcasts, in certain conditions; and when the set is properly tuned in, a force is exerted which generates neuro-muscular energy of the kind that can be seen working on the dowser's twig."

Even if this idea is accepted, the whole question is made more complex and difficult to grasp by the strange ability many dowsers possess of tracing the whereabouts of underground water or minerals from a map. By holding their dowsing instrument over a plan of an area, they are able to get accurate responses, which afterward are verified on the site. Since the map itself could not give off the radiations, we must look for a further explanation. Perhaps the map helps the dowser to focus his responses, and so pick up the radiations from the area shown in the map in a way that we are at present unable to understand. An analogy might be seen in the work of Edgar Cayce. He only needed the name and address of a patient to be able to tune in to him, however many miles away, to visualize his surroundings, and to diagnose his complaint. He was only able to do this while in trance, when there was no interference from his conscious mind. Dowsers also seem to be using some sixth sense or faculty outside the normal human range of consciousness. We may tend to dismiss this power because it is so outside our everyday experience, but our ancestors would have dismissed radio, television, and space flights in just the same way.

When prospecting for minerals, some dowsers carry small samples of the mineral with them. Whether this acts as an actual guide or merely serves to concentrate the dowser's faculties, rather like the map, is not clear. However, in the 19th century it was discovered that dowsers could distinguish between pure and polluted water, and dowsers made use of different samples of water to help them establish the different reactions to the different impurities. From this it was only a short step to using the dowsing instruments, most often the pendulum, for medical diagnosis to distinguish between healthy and unhealthy parts of the body. A pendulum swung over a healthy organ would have one reaction; swung over an unhealthy organ it would have a different reaction. In this way it was often possible to locate the source of various complaints. Some practitioners went further and used the technique to suggest remedies. Samples of different remedies, usually homeopathic, were held by the operator, and the pendulum was swung over the patient's body until a certain movement of the pendulum indicated that the correct medicine to use had been found.

The Abbe Mermet, who used the term *radiesthesia* to describe diagnosis with a pendulum, did much in France at the end of the 19th century to give these ideas respectability. He was a highly regarded member of the Church, and his careful scientific studies did much to put the work on a firm footing. His ideas were taken up and practiced in France and Italy, and gained an acceptance they have never enjoyed in either England or America. The Abbe Mermet himself often assisted the police in tracing missing persons. All he needed was an article belonging to the missing person that had not been excessively handled by other people. This was believed to contain the person's unique radiations, and could be used as a guide in finding the right response to the person who was missing from the pendulum.

Radiesthesia received an impetus from the research and

Above: an Irish businessman, Andrew Beasley, dowsing with the bent copper wire that serves him as a divining rod. Beasley lives in a farming community where cattle or sheep may stray from home. Using his rod and a map of the area, Beasley often can locate lost animals—and people as well. Left: like many dowsers, Beasley makes a preliminary search for his objective using a map in comfort at home. Later he goes out to the site for confirmation.

Abbé Mermet's Pendulum at Work

In 1933 a little six-year-old boy vanished from his home in Miège in the Swiss Alps. After an unsuccessful search for the boy, the town's mayor wrote to Abbé Mermet, who had often assisted police in locating missing people. The Abbé needed an article used by the missing person, a description of the last place he or she was seen, and a map of the surrounding area to do his work. He used a pendulum and a form of dowsing to find the missing person.

After the Abbé applied his pendulum to the problem of the missing boy, he reported that the child had been carried away into the mountains by a large bird of prey, probably an eagle. He also said that the bird— although enormous — had dropped its load twice to rest and regain its strength.

There was no trace of the boy at the first place the Abbé indicated. A recent heavy snowfall prevented a thorough search at the second place, but the conclusion was that Abbé Mermet had made a mistake.

When the snow melted two weeks later, however, a gang of woodcutters found the torn and mangled body of a small boy. It was the missing child. The bird had apparently been prevented from completely savaging the child's body by the sudden heavy storm that had also hidden the forlorn evidence.

Scientific investigation established that the boy's shoes and clothes had not come into contact with the ground where the body was found. He could only have reached the remote spot by air—the pitiful victim of the bird of prey. Later the boy's father apologized to the Abbé for having doubted him.

experiments of Albert Abrams, an eminent neurologist who was born in San Francisco in 1863. He had studied extensively in Europe under some of the greatest scientists of the time and, most unusual for a medical specialist, had acquired a knowledge of the newest developments in modern physics. Much of his later research was to be governed by an attempt to reconcile the laws of physics with those of biology. On his return to San Francisco he embarked on a brilliant medical career, achieving an international reputation and making many important contributions in his own field of neurology. But his work also had its unorthodox side. In 1898 the French scientists Pierre and Marie Curie had discovered the radioactive element radium, and Abrams soon became interested in the nature of radioactivity and the use of radium in the treatment of patients. A chance examination of a patient early in the century set him off on a long line of research which lasted until his death in 1924. It laid the foundation for what at first was known as the Electronic Reactions of Abrams, or ERA, and later became established as radionics.

The patient who set off this chain of research was a middle-aged man suffering from a chronic ulcer on his lip—technically known as an *epithelioma*, a form of cancer. While giving him a thorough checkup Abrams discovered that one small area in the region of the man's stomach sounded dull instead of hollow when tapped. What puzzled him was that it only sounded dull when the man faced west. If he faced any other direction or lay down on a couch, that small area of the body gave the normal hollow note.

Abrams' guess was that this puzzle had some connection with the earth's magnetic field, and he embarked on a program of research to solve this biophysical mystery. He examined other people suffering from the early stages of cancer, as well as those in good health and those suffering from numerous other diseases. His findings led him to the conclusion that when a patient faced west, the atoms in the diseased tissue emanated some kind of radiation that affected certain groups of nerve fibers. These then produced the muscular contractions he was able to hear as a dulled sound in certain parts of a patient's body. When he found that the different sounding points were specific to each disease, he realized the diagnostic value of his discovery. A dull note just below the navel, for instance, indicated the presence of tuberculosis; the place for detecting the presence of malaria was located to the left of the navel, and so on.

Right: the Abbé Mermet in one of the last photographs taken before his death in 1937. Mermet coined the term "radiesthesia" to describe diagnosis by dowsing, and his book *Principles and Practices of Radiesthesia* is the classic text on the subject. Mermet was honored in his own time, and among those who came to him for consultation was the Pope. He showed a great interest in Mermet's work.

Other discoveries were to follow. He placed a small container holding a cancer specimen against the forehead of a healthy young man. Within two seconds the hollow note Abrams had been obtaining from the subject's abdomen became dull. When the cancer specimen was removed the normal hollow note of health returned. Evidently the radiation from diseased tissue could affect a person's reactions even though the tissue did not come from his own body. Later, when he began to construct machines to help in diagnosis, Abrams also discovered that a drop of blood from a patient gave as definite a reading as a piece of tissue. Today practitioners in radionics generally use blood spots for convenience sake. The spots are sometimes called "witnesses."

Gradually Abrams began to formulate a theory to account for the astonishing results of his experiments. Long before it was a generally accepted fact, he concluded that radiation was a universal property of matter. He then went on to argue that if matter and energy were indistinguishable at the atomic level, the basis of disease was electronic and not cellular. If, as seemed to be apparent from his experiments, healthy and diseased tissue gave out different radiations, then it should be possible to build equipment to receive and diagnose these radiations, somewhat on the lines of a radio receiving set. It ought also to be possible to construct equipment on the same lines to treat and cure abnormal radiations, he believed.

In order to distinguish the different types of radiation emitted by different diseases, Abrams used an old-fashioned variable resistance box. This was the first of the notorious "magic boxes."

This was not Abrams' name for them, of course. He called them *reflexophones*. Later more refined versions were known as *sphygmobiometers* or *sphygmophones*. They were used principally for diagnosis. To cure the patient Abrams invented the *oscilloclast*, which is often known as the "black box." Its aim

Below: the especially designed and patented pendulum used by the Abbé to diagnose sickness and locate missing persons, among other feats based on dowsing. Sample substances can be put in the section that unscrews.

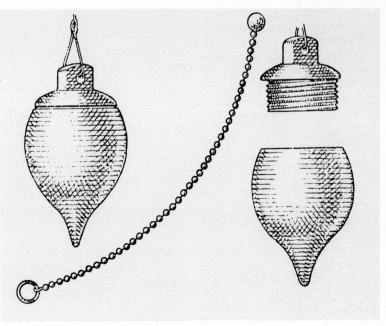

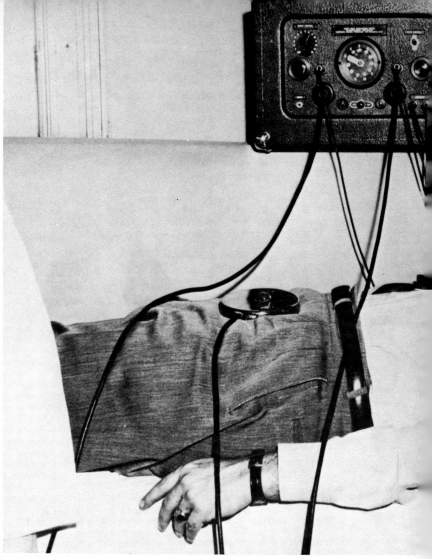

Above: Albert Abrams was born to a wealthy San Francisco family, and qualified at medical school before he was legally of age to receive his diploma. Instead he went to Europe for extensive postgraduate studies. He later specialized in diseases of the nervous system, and carried out research on spinal therapeutics.

was to produce measured vibrations that would destroy infection in the patient.

One of Abrams' early students, Dr. Eric Perkins, recalls an incident during a postgraduate course on Abrams' methods. Another doctor on the course was beginning to suffer from chest pains, and asked Abrams to diagnose in front of the class. Abrams warned him that the results of an examination were sometimes embarrassing, but the doctor told him to go ahead. It wasn't, he said, as though he was the least likely to have a venereal disease.

From the blood sample Abrams immediately got a strong reaction for syphilis. When he revealed this the doctor became very angry. "That's all bunk!" he shouted. "I don't care what your readings say! I tell you I've never had it!"

This incensed Abrams. "My work's all bunk, is it?" he growled. "I'll tell you if you caught it from a male or female and the site of the inoculation."

According to Perkins, the dials of the machine were then set to "sex combination." Abrams tapped both sides of his reluctant patient's abdomen and got a dull note on what he designated as the male side.

"He caught it from a male," Abrams announced. "Now we

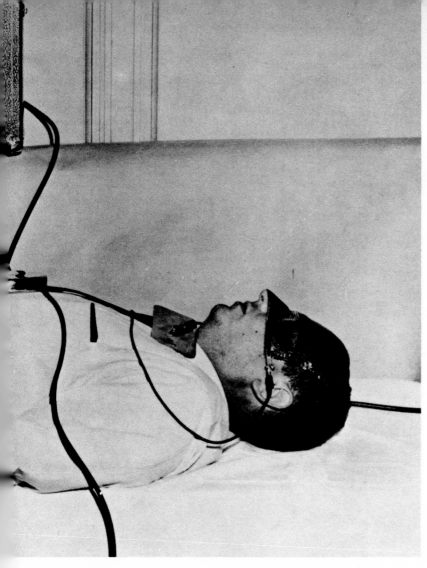

Left: a patient being treated by
means of vibration frequency
from a portable modern version of
Abrams' original "black box." This
box was designed for treatment;
others of Abrams' boxes were only
to be used to make a diagnosis.

have to find where he caught it. Let's try the hands first—
medical men often get infected on the hands."

Once again the angry doctor was examined, this time on his
hands where an electrode from the machine was pointed at
each finger in turn. Abrams got a reaction from the end of the
middle finger of the left hand and there, on inspection, he
found a scar.

"You've got me, Doctor Abrams!" confessed his patient.
"I jabbed that finger with a needle when sewing up a man after
an operation, and it did not heal for a long time. I never thought
it was a chancre."

With an electrode held over the man's chest Abrams diagnosed syphilitic aortitis as the cause of the chest pains. Fortunately, he was able to be reassuring about the prospects of a
cure provided treatment began at once.

Without Abrams' box the condition might well have remained undiagnosed for a considerably longer time.

Great interest was aroused by such diagnoses and by
treatments suggested by the machine and successfully carried
out. Patients and doctors flocked to San Francisco to study the
ERA. Upton Sinclair, the celebrated American novelist,
called Abrams' laboratory a "House of Wonders."

Interest was also aroused in Britain, and in 1924 a committee of the British Medical Association was appointed to investigate the phenomenon. Sir Thomas Horder, later the king's physician, was in the chair. Among medical circles it was confidently expected that the demonstrations arranged for the committee would be a failure, and ERA dismissed as a fraud. The succinct report quoted by Brian Inglis in *Fringe Medicine* is worth repeating. It said:

"The Committee's report was startling. Tests, it said, had been arranged under suitable supervision; the results had been carefully evaluated; and the Committee had come to the conclusion that 'no more convincing exposition of the reality of the phenomena could reasonably be desired.' Not merely was it satisfied that the claims about the diagnostic value of the method were proven: two of its members, Horder being one, had actually felt an alteration in their abdominal muscles at the time when—if the therapeutic claims are to be believed—they should have expected to feel them. As they had not been told what to expect, this could not have been from suggestion—not, at least, on a conscious level."

This seemed like a clear endorsement for Abrams. Unfortunately, however, the demonstration was conducted by Dr. W. E. Boyd of Glasgow who used a machine of his own called an *emanometer*. This was a development of the Abrams box, and Boyd was always careful to acknowledge his debt to Abrams. But the difference enabled the BMA committee to maintain that they were examining a different box entirely. Horder even made a point of criticizing all who employed the "scientifically unsound" paraphernalia of Abrams.

Thus the committee managed to praise and dismiss Abrams' work in the same statement. Orthodox medicine was able to interpret these findings as a general condemnation. Abrams himself died about this time—some say of a broken heart—and further development of his ideas slowed down.

Not for long, however. Ruth Beymer Drown, a chiropractor who had been Abrams' secretary, kept the infant science alive in the difficult period after its inventor's death. She began to devise new instruments and soon discarded external currents in her machines, believing that her task was to focus the life force which she held was present in everything. "It cannot be too strongly stressed," she wrote, "that the individual's own body energy is the only force or current used by the Drown Method in diagnosis, remedy selection, or treatment." She used the same instruments for diagnosing and treating, but in different ways. For diagnosis, the machine received and dealt with energy emanating from the diseased part of the body. For treatment, on the other hand, the whole of the body's energy was channeled through vibrations to act on the diseased part.

Ruth Drown was the first to regularly treat patients at a distance by means of a blood spot or other specimen. Abrams had found that a patient's blood spot gave off all the radiation necessary for diagnosing a disease. Ruth Drown applied this by using the blood spot as a way of tuning in with the distant patient. The right vibrations were focused on the blood spot, and it was held that these would be picked up by the patient.

Above: Ruth B. Drown. Trained as a chiropractor, she worked at the Abrams Clinic and set herself to improve Abrams' instruments. She was successful with most of her patients, but less so with her coworkers because of her policy of keeping details of her treatment secret. She would tell a coworker what treatment was necessary, but not how she had arrived at the right calculation. However, she is still revered as the martyr of radionics because of her imprisonment for fraud.

Ruth Drown built up a large practice in the 1930s and 40s. She also worked out a list of treatment rates for most parts of the body and nearly all the ailments that can afflict it. These treatment rates were based on the number and intensity of vibrations applied by the Drown machine to cure bodily disorders. In 1950 her supporters persuaded her to demonstrate the power of her instruments at the University of Chicago. Ten blood specimens were given to her, but her diagnosis of the first three was so inaccurate that she did not continue with the test. The following year the Food and Drugs Administration (FDA) arranged for her arrest on charges of fraud and medical quackery. Despite the bulk of evidence presented in her defense she was sentenced and her instruments seized and destroyed. Shortly afterward she died. Practitioners of radionics look on her as their first—and it is hoped their only—martyr.

The practice of radionics is still a technically illegal act in the United States. The English author and editor Edward W. Russell wrote to the FDA in 1973 to ascertain their current attitude. He was told in effect that since they were required to ensure that all devices were "safe, effective, and properly labeled" they knew "of no way of labeling a device so that it would bear adequate directions for use for Radionic Medicine."

Investigation into radionics is now concentrated in Britain—although it may also be taking place in the Soviet Union where there is vigorous research into all manifestations of parapsychology. The diagnostic instruments most used in Britain are those designed by George de la Warr in his Oxford laboratories. During World War II de la Warr was asked to copy one of the Drown instruments for someone who was unable to obtain it. His interest in radionics was immediately aroused, and he began to devote most of his time and energy to experimenting and researching in the field. He was the first to produce standardized, highly accurate instruments. Working in close cooperation with his wife Marjorie, he devised a new diagnostic instrument. It resembled a large portable radio with nine tuning knobs. Blood spots or other samples were placed in two small cups above the knobs. A master index of 5000 rates was compiled by testing different diseases. To diagnose a sample the knobs were tuned until the correct rate was found. This could then be indentified by checking against the index. The method of determining the rate was a strange one, with some similarities to dowsing. A thin rubber membrane was fixed to the base of the instrument. The operator would rotate the dials and stroke the membrane. Most of the time there was no reaction, but if the rubber became sticky, it meant that some of the dials were tuned to a correct rate. Confirmation or more details could be obtained by further tuning. After diagnosis the patient would be treated with specific remedies, by a treatment instrument, or both. To use the treatment instrument, the complementary rate to the diagnosis was worked out, the machine tuned in to the patient's blood spot, and treatment broadcast through the ether to distant patients. In 1960 an action in the High Court was brought against the de la Warrs by a dissatisfied purchaser of a machine. However, they were cleared of all charges of fraud and their honesty and sincerity

Above: George de la Warr, who continued Ruth Drown's work, began by duplicating one of her instruments. He and his wife devised new radionic instruments for both diagnosis and treatment.

was publicly established by what came out in their trial.

The successful radionics practitioner has to have some of the talents of a dowser and be sensitive to ESP, but the Delawarr Laboratories estimate that six people out of ten are able to operate the box to some extent, and three of those six can do so extremely well. The chief drawback is that the operator's ability can be disturbed by certain states of mind. The presence of a skeptic is said to be inhibiting, but nervousness also has a damaging effect.

Several mocking tales are told about radionics. One recounts the hoax played on Abrams by a Michigan doctor who sent in a blood sample from a Plymouth Rock rooster, and got back a diagnosis of malaria, cancer, diabetes, and two venereal diseases. But radionics has continued to have its successes, and our knowledge of the life force—by whatever name we choose to call it—is still so incomplete that it is unwise to dismiss any method which seeks to understand it.

The history of healing is filled with examples of methods used for healing before the principles by which they operated were known. Color therapy from the 13th century provides a notable case. When a son of King Edward I caught smallpox, the royal physician, John of Gaddesden, hung red cloth all around his bed. By doing so he reduced the disfiguring effect of pitting considerably. John of Gaddesden may have had mystical reasons for choosing the color red, but the treatment worked. Nearly 600 years were to pass before Niels Finsen, the Danish pioneer of phototherapy, showed that the success of the

Above: Marjorie de la Warr, who has carried on her husband's work since his death in 1969. A dedicated radionic practitioner, she has often told her students that the sole object of the practitioner must be to get the patient well by the quickest and most appropriate treatment—whether that be radionics or not.

treatment was the result of preventing ultraviolet light from reaching the patient's skin.

In cases other than smallpox, the beneficial effect of the full spectrum of the sun's ray are well known. Deprived of sunlight the body is unable to convert the fat present in the skin into Vitamin D. The effect of different colors on illness is still the subject of experimental tests, but already it is thought advisable that the colors red and orange should not be used in mental wards—however cheerful they may appear to visitors. Some colortherapists irradiate their patients with light shining through colored glass, and claim that certain colors and color combinations are of benefit to definite diseases—yellow for indigestion, blue for skin troubles, violet for ease in childbirth, for instance. Finsen showed that a tubercular condition of the skin, known as lupus, is improved when subjected to ultraviolet rays.

As with rays of light, so with sound. Music has been used in healing since ancient times. Sounds and music were thought to be of magic origin, and could therefore communicate directly with the spirits. The music played by the witch doctor or medicine man was not designed to calm or comfort the patient, but to break the resistance of the spirit by means of its own magic power. Juliette Alvin, a professional cellist and founder in 1958 of the British Society for Music Therapy, explains that while the beat of "magic music" can seem monotonous, the music in fact goes through different emotional moods as it tries to persuade, flatter, cajole, or threaten the evil spirit

The Delawarr Laboratories manufacture standard instruments for diagnosis and treatment, and will also custom build such machines from an individual's own design. It is always stressed in radionics, however, that the instruments are not automatic. It needs a skilled and sensitive operator to take advantage of radionic principles. Below left: the basic instrument for diagnosis of disease and for research and agricultural application. A blood spot is being put into a specimen well for analysis. This model is nonelectrical.

Below right: one of the radionic instruments used for treatment.

responsible for disease to go away and leave the patient cured.

In biblical times we find David the harp player calming the madness of Saul. Greek and Arab medicine recommended soothing songs and the playing of flutes for certain complaints. To treat sciatica musicians played close to the patient's body to make his flesh move. The Greek mathematician Pythagoras used loud music to treat mental patients, calling this his "musical medicine." The voice has also been used for this purpose, notably by the great 18th-century Neapolitan singer Farinelli. In 1737 he paid a visit to Spain where he found the moody and melancholy King Philip V suffering another of his lengthy depressions. He was hiding away from his court—unshaven, slovenly, and slumped in lethargy. The Queen invited Farinelli to sing in an adjoining room, and asked him to choose some of his more expressive and poignant songs. Farinelli sang four, including one entitled *Pallido il sole—Pale is the Sun*. These expressed the King's melancholy so perfectly that he emerged from his depression and resumed the business of state upon hearing them. Farinelli remained in Spain until King Philip's death nine years later. Every evening the King asked him to sing the same four plaintive and melodic songs and no others.

A unique form of madness raged in Southern Italy toward the end of the Middle Ages for which the only cure seemed to be music, and only a certain kind of fast music. The madness centered around the ancient town of Taranto in the Apulian heel of southern Italy. It was said to be caused by the bite of a local spider, the tarantula. The madness was therefore named tarantism, and the frantic music that caused the people to dance wildly until they were cured was called the tarantella.

In the intense summer heat a peasant would suddenly jump up, cry out that a spider had bitten him, and run to the market place. There he would find other sufferers lying slumped by the roadside while neighbors desperately searched the countryside for musicians to come and play the tarantella. Bands of musicians wandered the countryside throughout the summer for this very purpose, carrying violins, pipes, and small drums. They played the tarantella, repeating the same tune again and again. Gradually sufferers would revive and move a limb. Then they started to dance faster and faster, going through the night and even the following day until they dropped exhausted and the madness was cured.

One strange feature of the disease was that people's madness returned year after year on the anniversary of the bite, whereupon they would have to repeat their frenzied dancing. Other things were puzzling too. If a tarantula was taken out of Apulia its bite became harmless. What was special about Apulia?

The probable explanation is that the wild dancing was an essential safety valve, a hysterical release of energies pent up by the miseries and fears of medieval life. As to why it should occur in Apulia and nowhere else, here is one interesting explanation. Pythagoras went to Apulia with his musical medicine in the 6th century B.C., and lived in Taranto until his death. Christianity was slow to take root in the far south of Italy, and it is thought that the orgiastic rites of Bacchus, the god of wine, celebrated in

Above: Niels Ryberg Finsen, the pioneer of phototherapy. He discovered that ultraviolet radiation on lupus and other skin afflictions brought about cures. Below: patients in Denmark under the Finsen ultraviolet radiation treatment for skin tuberculosis. Finsen received the Nobel Prize.

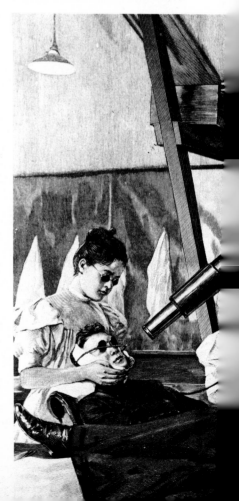

Pythagoras' time, probably survived in secret—to reemerge into the light of day as the dancing madness of Apulia in the Middle Ages.

Tarantism faded away in the 17th century and is now extinct. It had served its purpose. But many people today still have little tolerance for strange ideas and practices that they do not understand, even if the practices do no harm and they themselves are not directly affected by them. Five years after the arrest of Ruth Drown the FDA moved against a more celebrated figure, the internationally known therapist Wilhelm Reich.

Since Reich's death in a prison hospital in 1957, the last years of his life have become encrusted with legend. To the young generation his work is expressed in the slogan, "Make Love Not War." The connection of this slogan with his ideas is aided by the titles of his most significant books, *The Sexual Revolution* and *The Function of the Orgasm*. He is seen as a forerunner of the Permissive Society.

Reich believed that virtually all mental disturbances and a great many physical illnesses are the result of sexual repression in infancy and in puberty. Men and women become trapped within a "character armor" of unhealthy submissions and resentment. This armor expresses itself in muscular rigidity, tensions, and stereotyped facial expressions. Reich's novel approach to his patients was to draw attention to these repeatedly, and this appears to have had considerable success as a means of uncovering some of their childhood crises. Even the many psychotherapists who feel that Reich stressed the effects

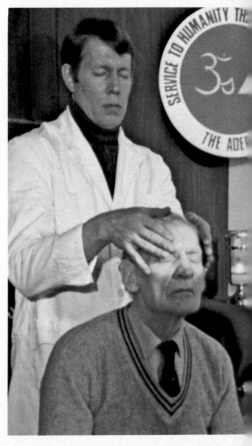

Below: color therapy by the Aetherius Society in London. The color green is reported to be related to emotional troubles, circulatory and heart ailments, headaches, and other allied ills. Generally, various shades of a color are used for treatment.

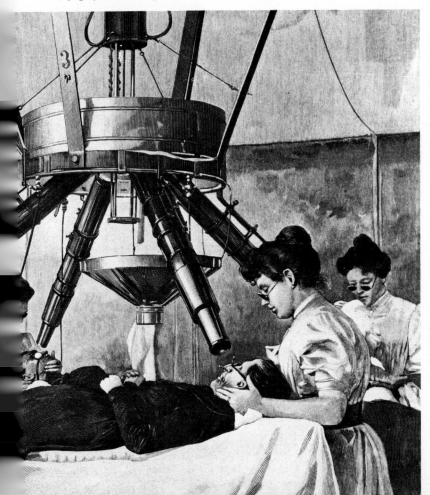

of sexual repression to the neglect of other factors admire his work on character analysis. It is largely through his influence that many therapists discarded the role of anonymous wise man and reach out to a patient as one human being to another.

More controversial are his views on sexual energy. According to Reich a man or woman imprisoned within a character armor becomes unable to discharge sexual energy completely during orgasm. Unexpressed sexual energy emerges as neurotic symptoms, anxiety, and sadism, making the person less able to achieve satisfactory orgasm the next time. The process continues in a vicious circle.

Reich uses the word orgasm to express more than is commonly meant. The individual must "surrender to the flow of biological energy without any inhibition. There must be no trace of sadism in the male nor of masochism in the female, no smug satisfaction in the male, no talking either, except words of tenderness, and no laughing." In *The Function of the Orgasm* he describes the "orgiastically satisfying sexual act" in great detail. Coming as it did six years before the Kinsey Report and its startling revelations of American sex habits, it was an undertaking of some courage.

According to Reich, very few individuals achieve full orgiastic potency. All neurotics and most civilized people fail. But the importance of achieving it lay in the fact that Reich identified sexual energy with the life force, present throughout Nature

Below: Wilhelm Reich, therapist and psychoanalyst, in 1955, two years before his death. It was at this time that he was being investigated by the Food and Drug Administration because of his famous orgone boxes, which he claimed could cure cancer.

Right: a still from the Yugoslav film *W.R.: Mysteries of the Organism.* It was a loosely plotted tribute to Reich based in large part on his controversial theories.

128

and filling the Universe. He called this force "primordial cosmic energy" or "orgone energy." He claimed to have observed the units of this energy—called "bions"—under a microscope and detected them by Geiger counter. The spots we sometimes see in front of our eyes are said to be examples of it. He believed that cancer is caused by bions which had degenerated through stagnation.

Reich fell foul of the FDA when he declared that orgone energy could be stored in boxes, known as orgone energy accumulators. These boxes, about the size of narrow telephone booths or coffins were made of steel encased in wood. They were said to act like greenhouses, letting in the orgone energy and storing and concentrating it. The sick were to sit within the boxes to be irradiated with orgone energy. By these means Reich claimed to be able to cure cancer. For these ideas and practices, he was arrested, imprisoned, and his books destroyed.

There is today no scientific agreement about the radiation said to be detected by diagnostic boxes, or the energy stored in accumulation boxes. Nor is there certainty that the life force in man can be identified with any force that fills the Universe and moves the stars. But a belief in a life force of some kind is central to many successful methods of healing. If its existence has not yet been proved, it may be because scientific instruments are simply not sensitive enough for the task. The end of this particular story lies in the future.

Below: the interior of one of Reich's orgone boxes. It is a wooden structure lined with metal. The idea was that the boxes were constructed so that they trapped orgone in the way a greenhouse traps sunlight: the energy can enter through the walls in this case, but once inside cannot be released. Thus the boxes were supposed to accumulate orgone energy for therapeutic use.

8

The Way Ahead

The study of healing without medicine reveals a rich variety of opinion on the causes of ill-health and how to treat it. One belief maintains that sickness results from a disturbance in the balance of Yin and Yang, another that it expresses the anger of the gods. A third claims that the bones of the spine have pinched a blood vessel, a fourth blames waste products in the blood, a fifth points to a discolored aura. A sixth . . . but the list is endless. For those open-minded enough to look outside the boundaries of conventional medicine the picture, unfortunately, is bewildering. Do all the different theories merit equal consideration, or is it

The course of our century has been far from an untroubled one, and the speed of our civilization and the demands it makes on us have contributed to a great deal of vaguely defined illness which orthodox medicine has often been unable to treat with unqualified success. For many, the answer has been to turn to unorthodox methods of care and healing—trusting in amazingly varied theories to find health and peace. Right: the *Distressed Man*, a painting by the American artist Ben Shahn in 1963. Stress has been called the 20th-century disease.

"The psychosomatic need for symptoms can be carried to extraordinary lengths"

reasonable to be selective on the basis of cultural background and personal inclination? If one chooses an idea that appears to be sound and to have produced good results, does this mean rejecting all the other ideas, many of which may seem to be equally convincing and to have produced equally good results? Above all, does it mean totally discarding the treatment offered by ordinary medicine?

When a situation is as complex as this, it is often helpful to look at it from a different angle. In place of the question, "What is the cause of illness?" we might examine whether some illnesses exist because they serve a purpose. The question can then be phrased, "Does illness meet a need we may have?" At first sight this question may seem like nonsense. Nobody, after all, wants to be ill. Or do they? Research into the onset of stress diseases and psychosomatic disorders shows that in many cases the answer to this is a definite "Yes." The German analyst Georg Groddeck was known as the father of psychosomatic medicine. In 1917 he published a paper in which he denied the commonly held assumption that only hysterics had the power to make themselves ill. He insisted that everyone had this ability, and often used it without realizing it to serve a definite purpose, such as avoiding a frightening situation. He believed that many so-called miraculous cures stemmed from the patients' sudden realization that they no longer needed the protection of the illness, and were able to face their own problems and cope with them.

An example among famous personalities was that of the English poet Elizabeth Barrett. A serious spinal injury in her teens confined her to bed for several years. Her general health was so affected that she was regarded as a permanent invalid, and she rarely left her sickroom. However, it is now thought that her illness may have been a way of escaping from her exceptionally tyrannical and demanding father. For in the spring of 1846 she met Robert Browning, and in the autumn, at the age of 40, she was able to leave her couch to marry him secretly. They went to Italy, where she even climbed mountains. At 43 she bore a healthy son. In the light of present-day knowledge of psychology, one might conclude that she no longer needed her illness.

A familiar figure in many offices is the man who suffers severe colds whenever the pressure of work becomes too much. He is not shamming. His nose streams, his eyes gum up, he gets a temperature. How many headaches—genuine headaches caused by alterations in the flow of blood to the head—are suffered by one of the marriage partners who does not want to go out to dinner!

The psychosomatic need for symptoms can be carried to extraordinary lengths. In the 1930s two doctors from Indiana, G. D. Bivin and M. P. Klinger, studied 444 cases of false pregnancy. All the symptoms of pregnancy were present—morning sickness, gradual swelling of abdomen and breasts, suspension of menstruation. In many of the women the condition lasted a full nine months, and in 138 cases labor pains occurred.

Symptoms of syphilis can be produced by a man who feels guilty about sleeping with a woman not his wife. False venereal disease symptoms are remarkably common in such situations. In fact doctors have a saying that the letters G.C. refer to two kinds of veneral trouble: the first is gonococcus, the bacterium causing gonorrhoea, and the other is guilty conscience.

Pasteur's discoveries in microbiology in the 1850s heralded an era in which doctors came to accept that there was a specific physical cause for each disease, and that in time a specific physical cure would be found. For example, it was found that syphilis was caused by the microorganism *spirichaeta pallida*. In 1910 the German chemist Paul Ehrlich produced the drug Salversan, which was able to destroy the spirochaetes. The assumption was that it was only a matter of time before "specifics"—as particular cures for particular diseases are called—were discovered for all infection. It was also believed that cures for degenerative diseases would follow the same pattern so that cancer, rheumatoid arthritis, and such, would eventually be conquered through them. But since the discovery of Salversan the search for specifics has, in many ways, been disappointing. Advances have been made, of course, but many new drugs have been found to have unfortunate side effects or, as happened in the case of Salversan itself, the germs have developed a new strain resistant to a particular drug.

In the meantime, however, much has been learned about the power of the mind over the body and the remarkable way in which the body can produce physical symptoms of ill health through suggestion, either conscious or unconscious. Hypnotism provides several examples, one of the most impressive being the burn-blister that a cold metal can produce on a subject's skin if he is told it is red-hot. There are many cases of people being struck

Below left: Elizabeth Barrett, the poet, in her bed. She was a complete invalid when she met and fell in love with Robert Browning.

Below: Robert Browning. After he and Elizabeth Barrett eloped, her health improved so much that three years later, living the life of a normal woman in Italy, she gave birth to a healthy son.

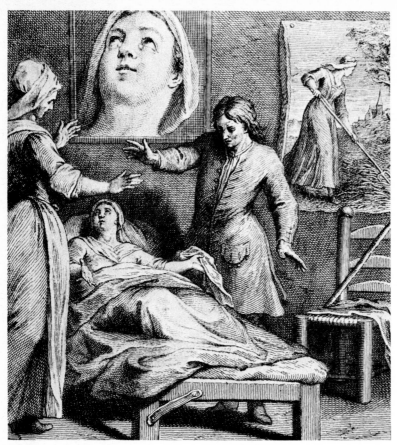

Left: one of the miraculous cures attributed to a visit to the tomb of a pious deacon in Paris. This peasant woman was cured of fistulas in her eyes, relieving her of almost unendurable pain. The scenes of convulsions at the tomb of the deacon got so out of hand that the authorities closed the cemetery entirely in 1732.

Below: Louis Pasteur in his laboratory. A chemist, Pasteur developed the theory that germs cause infection. This led medical research to try to find specific antidotes for specific germs as the way to combat diseases.

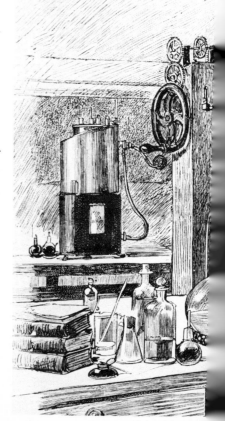

blind or dumb after an emotional shock or experience. Saul's attack of blindness on the road to Damascus is a classic example from the Bible. Another is the way in which certain saints and other devout Christians have developed the five wounds of Christ, known as the stigmata, on their bodies. The Roman Catholic church is well aware that the great majority of cures attributed to shrines and relics are hysterical rather than miraculous. This is not to deny that they are genuine, however, for if the body can make itself ill there is no reason why it cannot also make itself well.

Of course our understanding of the power wielded by the mind over the body should not blind us to the great achievements of what may be called "mechanical" medicine. According to the mechanical view, a person is essentially a collection of organs and associated processes which can be regulated like a car, with the medical equivalents for oiling it, adjusting the connections, replacing worn parts, and letting it run at low revs for a few days. This mechanical outlook was an essential stage in the development of medical knowledge, and led to great understanding of the workings of the body. As a result of its achievements and the development of public hygiene, the expectancy of life in America and Western Europe is 20 years longer today than in 1900. But in emphasizing the mechanical view of the body, too much was excluded—notably the emotions. Dr. F. G. Crookshank, a British pioneer of the study of stress diseases, rebelled against the mechanical theory in the 1920s, saying: "I often wonder that some hardboiled and orthodox clinician does not describe emotional weeping as a 'new disease,' calling it paroxysmal lachrymation, and suggesting treatment by belladonna, astringent local applications, avoidance of sexual excess, tea, tobacco and alcohol, and a salt-free diet with restrictions on fluid intake, proceeding in the event of failure to early removal of the tear glands!"

The limitations of the mechanical view can be seen in the case of allergies, which are extreme and adverse reactions experienced by some people when brought into contact with certain substances. Until the last century asthma and hay fever had been traditionally assumed to be the effect of "nerves." That is to say, their cause was thought to be closely linked to the sufferer's emotional state. But at the turn of the century doctors studied allergies more closely. Sufferers from asthma and hay fever were tested to find out what substances caused an attack. Various offenders, such as pollen or cat's fur, were identified. Treatment was prescribed on the basis of this finding, and had good effect in many cases. But subsequent research showed that many of the people who gave a positive reaction to allergy tests in the laboratory never in fact suffered from allergic symptoms outside. Others whose hay fever developed when they smelled the pollen from certain flowers, sometimes developed it when they were in the presence of artificial flowers. In experiments at Cornell University patients were interviewed in a room that, without their knowledge, had been impregnated with the pollen to which they were allergic. They indicated no discomfort until the conversation turned to subjects they found emotionally disturbing, whereupon their hay fever symptoms developed. These disappeared when

Below: Paul Ehrlich. He fueled the hopes of eventual control of all disease with his formulation of a synthetic drug, Salversan, which destroyed the microorganism causing the dread disease syphilis.

Does an Allergy Cause Schizophrenia?

Allergies mean rashes, puffed eyes and running noses, and breathing difficulties. And they usually come from pollen or the less common foods such as shellfish or strawberries. At least that's how we think of it. Now a British doctor claims that allergies can bring on headaches, neuroses, and even severe mental illnesses like schizophrenia. And the source of these problems is everyday foods—sugar, white bread, and cereals for example.

Dr. Richard Mackarness, a psychiatrist who has been trying to prove his theory to the medical profession for the last 10 years, also believes that people get addicted to the very foods to which they are allergic. These are likely to be what a person likes best and eats most often. To test for allergy, he puts a patient on a five-day fast. If there is no immediate improvement in their condition, food allergy is not the cause. If there is an improvement, food allergy could be what is wrong. He then gives the patient small amounts of all suspect foods with a drop tester, putting the sample under the tongue. In this way the sample enters the blood stream quickly, reaching the brain in half a minute and bringing a bad reaction if it is one of the allergenic foods.

The most dramatic success Dr. Mackarness has had was with a woman who had been in and out of mental hospitals for seven years and had been given up as incurable. The doctor discovered the foods she was allergic to and changed her diet to exclude them. Within a week she was well enough to leave the hospital and get a job to support herself.

the conversation turned to something less personally troubling.

These investigations showed that people can suffer from hay fever even when there is no physical cause, and conversely that they may not suffer even when the usual physical cause is present. The significant feature in the Cornell study is that the symptoms were shown to develop when the physical and emotional causes were present together.

The emotions have a crucial effect on a disease that might be thought beyond the power of the mind to influence—cholera. Dr. A. T. W. Simeons, a British physician who practiced for some years in India, became aware of a curious fact concerning this dread disease. He describes this in a book published in 1960 called *Man's Presumptuous Brain*. He pointed out that usually in a cholera epidemic the very old and the very young survive. The chief victims are men and women in the prime of life—those whom one might expect to possess greater powers of resistance. Once again the explanation is to be found in the power of mind over matter. The cholera bacillus flourishes in an alkaline medium that, when taken into the body, is normally killed by stomach acids. But fear and worry can alter the rate of acid secretion from the stomach walls. When a cholera epidemic occurs, men and women in the prime of life are the ones who worry most. They are the wage earners, the heads of households, the ones who look after everyone else. By a tragic irony the worry, brought on by their sense of responsibility, alters the acid content of their stomachs enough to allow the cholera bacilli to slip through into the alkaline haven of the small intestine. There it flourishes with fatal results. The aged, who hardly care if they survive or not, and the babies ignorant of what is happening around them, continue to secrete stomach acid in the normal way. To this extent, cholera is a psychological disease.

A number of people are also coming to suspect that cancer, the great unsolved modern medical mystery, is significantly affected by the mind.

The orthodox approach to the understanding of cancer is to ask, "What substances cause it?" The reactions of humans—and rats or dogs or mice—are tested concerning all sorts of possible causes. A wide range of offenders has been isolated by these means—smoking, excess sugar, excess salt, excess meat, food additives, and diesel fumes are but a few. People can inherit a proneness to develop it but heredity, like smoking and the rest, is a physical factor. They are all the equivalent of Pasteur's microbe. Fresh insight might come from following Pasteur's deathbed advice to consider the *terrain*, the ground in which the microbe spreads. This ground is the nature of the patient.

Sir Heneage Ogilvie, former specialist at Guy's Hospital in London, made a plea for a different approach in the 1950s. Comparing the groups of cells in the human body to colonies within an empire, he pointed out that in aging empires colonies seek to go their own way.

"At 48," he said, "the individual cell groups tend to lose their corporate loyalty, to increase their numbers without any social need, and to make demands for nourishment which their neighbors cannot satisfy. The question 'why do so many of us get cancer after the age of 48?' has proved entirely sterile as a guiding

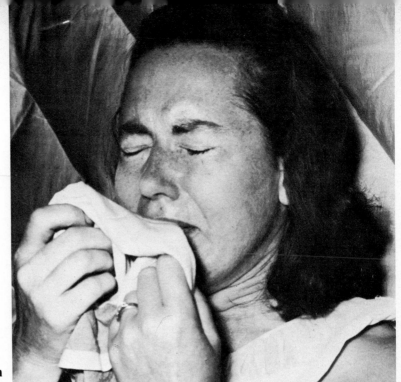

Right: the sneezes of a hay fever sufferer—with the accompanying miseries of itchy nose and eyes and general irritability—may well have some emotional basis underlying the physical reaction to several physical irritants.

Below: checking for allergies. Although in many cases finding the specific irritant solves the problem if that irritant can be avoided, doctors have discovered that in other patients the allergic condition continues. This indicates that there is more than a simply physical explanation for the patient's discomfort.

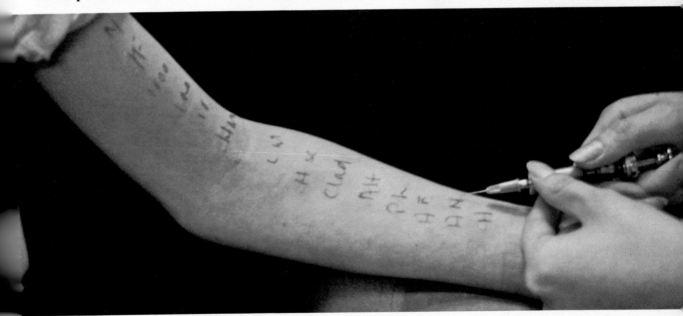

principle of research. It is surely time we posed and faced the real problem 'We all have cancer at 48. What is the force that keeps it in check in the great majority of us?'"

Ogilvie admitted that his maxim of "The happy man never gets cancer" may not be an inflexible rule but he went on to say: "The instances where the first recognizable onset of cancer has followed almost immediately on some disaster, a bereavement, the breakup of a relationship, a financial crisis, or an accident, are so numerous that they suggest that some controlling force that has hitherto kept this outbreak of cell communism in check has been removed."

It is possible that, as in the case of hay fever, the answer to cancer will be found in a combination of physical and emotional

137

causes, a deep-seated reaction that ultimately alters the behavior of cells. On the face of it, a transformation in a patient's emotional state would seem a likely explanation of why cancer sometimes stops developing or regresses for no reason that doctors can discover. For those who find themselves unable to believe in spirit guides and auras, some link between the emotions and cancer might supply an acceptable explanation for the cures claimed by faith healers.

Some support for this theory comes from the humble wart. Like cancer this affliction is an unwelcome growth on the human body—although unlike cancer it is harmless. It can be cured by suggestion. In fact, as Professor H. J. Eysenck showed in his experiments with schoolchildren, a treatment by suggestion using a magic picture of a child's warts is more effective than the orthodox medical treatment of burning them off with acid.

The great power of the mind has still to be fully appreciated. A story that illustrates this concerns a French professor who suffered a severe attack of asthma when spending the night in an unfamiliar hotel room. Knowing that his only hope of recovering breath was to find a source of fresh air, he staggered out of bed and groped his way to what he supposed to be the window. He searched in vain for the window catch and, not finding it, broke the glass in desperation. After standing there a few moments and gulping in the air, his asthma symptoms subsided and he was able to return to bed. He passed the remainder of the night at ease. The following morning he discovered that he had broken the glass front of an old grandfather clock, but the gulps of stale air from inside the case had been as effective as cool fresh air in controlling his symptoms.

This was one of the cases recorded by Emile Coué, a pharmacist from Nancy. Born in 1857, he developed the art of suggestion into a healing system. He described how, while still a poor student, he witnessed "the cure of an extremely refractory illness, when the patient, on his advice, took a new patent medicine. Greatly astonished at the result, he analyzed the medicine, and found it was a harmless compound whose whole value was based upon skillful puffery—and above all, upon the involuntary eloquence with which he himself had advised the use of the remedy, and upon the patient's confidence in him and his word."

A. A. Liébeault was working in Nancy at this time, curing the local peasants by hypnosis. Coué studied his methods and came to the conclusion that the curing power lay not in the hypnotist but in the patient. He reasoned that the presence of the hypnotist would not be needed if some way could be found of triggering off the patient's power to cure himself.

The system he evolved, which he called autosuggestion, was extremely simple and designed to exploit the unconscious imagination of the patient. He instructed his patients to repeat to themselves many times a day, but especially early in the morning and late in the evening, a little phrase which was designed to put them in the right emotional frame of mind. He devised several of these, but the most famous one was, "Every day in every way I am getting better and better." It was not the actual words that mattered but the emotional feeling that they engendered.

The phrase worked like magic. In a sense it was magic. People

Above: Émile Coué, the French psychotherapist whose theories led hundreds of thousands of people all over the world to begin their day with the hopeful formula, "Every day in every way I am getting better and better."

came away from his free clinic murmuring the little phrase—and they were cured of asthma, skin diseases, paralysis, and even appendicitis, which was the fashionable complaint of the period.

Coué's methods may appear to resemble the modern method of positive thinking, but this latter method aims to discipline the will power into ordering the body to be healthy. It takes no account of the fact that an unconscious wish to be ill may be present. In such cases positive thinking will only work until the unconscious, like a dammed stream, finds a route around the obstructing will and expresses itself in some other form—not necessarily as illness, but maybe as ill-temper or clumsiness or failure. Coué opposed any idea of coercion. His method was designed to have a direct effect on the unconscious by bypassing the will. This was why the favored times for repeating the phrases were morning and evening, when the unconscious was most receptive and relaxed. Coué died in 1926. In the 1920s his ideas were practiced by people all over the world, but their popularity seemed to die out with Coué's own death.

Human beings are capable of being cured by almost anything providing they believe it will cure them. This fact has been discovered by those attempting to test new drugs, and has been learned to their cost. One method of attempting to evaluate the effects of a new drug is to take two equally balanced groups of subjects. One group is given the drug and the second group, the control, is given a harmless substance said to be the drug. The drug substitute is usually made from sugar, and is known as a *placebo* from the Latin meaning "I will please." The idea of the control group is for the experimenters to have some standard of comparison so that it can be seen what happens to a sick person who is given treatment as opposed to one who is not. Unfortunately for the experimenters, a considerable number of the control subjects get better because they believe that they have been given treatment. The eloquence of the doctor, as Coué discovered, persuades the person that the drug will work, and in many cases the placebo proves as effective as the actual drug.

To counter this difficulty the "double blind" system has been devised. In this method not only the subject but also the doctor is kept in ignorance as to whether the pill administered is a new drug or a placebo. To the further confusion of the experimenters, there is still sometimes little difference in the effects. This makes one wonder whether it is the content of the medicine or the human attention that matters to the sick.

Appreciation of the power that the mind can exercise over the body makes it easier to understand what needs disease satisfies. Freud pointed out that if psychic energy is unable to satisfy itself in its original object it will fix upon an alternative object. This is the impulse that leads to sublimation. It can also lead to illness. Frustration seems to be the inescapable accompaniment of Western civilization, perhaps of all civilizations. The difficulties attendant on the child's feelings for its parents can be an early source of frustration. Sexual deprivation, the social pressure to conform, and the struggle for position are frustrations frequently met with in adulthood. The individual adapts himself to these as best he can, but if the pressures on him become too heavy or too persistent, he may move into a state of chronic stress. One

Magic and Modern Medicine

Is there still magic today in the whole idea of medicine? It would seem so from a study of *placebos*, which are harmless nonmedical substances prescribed to patients who expect to take medicine as part of their treatment. The astounding thing about sugar pills and other such placebos is that they often work: they help cure everything from coughs to mental disorders. For example, experiments have shown that over 30 percent of people suffering from coughs, colds, nausea, or tension felt better after taking a placebo—which, of course, they thought was real medicine when they took it.

American experiments have also shown that 35 percent of patients given a saline injection for post-operative pain responded well. Even 40 percent of angina sufferers felt relief from sharp pains upon taking a placebo.

Stranger still is the case of those who improve or get cured even though they *know* that what they are taking is medically without any value. In one case, a group of psychiatric patients knew they were taking nothing but sugar pills. Yet all felt considerably better after taking them for a period of two months.

One doctor maintains that many sick people feel better immediately if they are given some pills or a bottle of medicine. They may take only one or two doses, but they get a sense of security from knowing that they have the medicine handy—like having a lucky charm. He adds that the most effective placebos are colored, nasty in taste, and expensive. Whatever form the placebos take, however, they seem to work—like magic.

Above: the increasingly crowded conditions in which city dwellers live their lives create a special kind of stress of its own—and as the numbers on our planet remorselessly increase, many scientists and other concerned thinkers try to predict the effect upon the health of the individual and the life of the community as we now know it.

Right: *The Ulcer Life* by the artist Bob Sullivan. The many stresses and pressures of 20th-century urban life are suggested by the layers of nails pressing threateningly toward the subject.

effect of this is that the body becomes less able to fend off the onslaught of germs. The second damaging effect is that the individual may, unconsciously, find a way of turning his frustrated energy in on himself in the form of aches and disease.

An investigation conducted in Scotland in the 1950s by Dr. D. M. Kissen looked into the emotional condition of tuberculosis patients. The results showed a high incidence of "severe emotional stress" preceding the onset of their illness. As many as 90 per cent of the stresses could be grouped under the heading of "Break or serious threat of a break in a love link"—using the term "love" in its spiritual sense rather than in its sexual meaning.

About the same time as the Kissen experiment in Scotland, Dr. Franz Alexander in Chicago was finding that strong but inhibited aggressive impulses led to chronically increased muscle tension, and was a contributing factor in rheumatoid arthritis. When inhibited aggression was associated with anxiety it raised the blood pressure, as though the body "were constantly in preparation for a fight which never takes place." Alexander showed that high blood pressure is extremely uncommon in the African black, but frequent in the American black—the damaging effect of a more stressful environment.

The close relationship between stress and diabetes has also been pointed out. In a recent American study 20 out of 25 new diabetics were found to have suffered the loss of someone close to them or experienced some severe setback shortly before the symptoms developed. Ulcers are a familiar example of a stress disease, along with migraine and most intestinal problems.

In the opinion of Dr. F. G. Crookshank, "Every person who is ill is ill psychically as well as physically." To neglect this possibility is to fail the healing art. The only satisfactory method of curing illnesses is to uncover the repressed frustrations, fears, griefs, hatreds, and loves, to try to help the sick person come to terms with himself, and to divert his energies to more positive and appropriate channels. The better kind of old-fashioned family doctor could take note of the family situation of his patient because he knew the family well. He could adjust his treatment accordingly. The better kind of modern doctor is alert to the revealing tricks of the patient's reaction—the misstatements, the moistening of the lips, the evasions, the changes in color, the shifts in bodily posture. If he is true to his calling, he will take the time to get to the root of the problem, past the symptoms.

In the 16th century Paracelsus, standing on the threshold of alchemy and science, believed that the art of medicine rested on four pillars. Astronomy, the natural sciences, and chemistry made up three of these pillars. The fourth was love. Love or caring was a quality displayed by another important 16th-century medical figure. This was Ambroise Paré, chief physician to the Court of France during the long turbulent regime of Catherine de'Medici. Moved to pity by the sufferings of ordinary soldiers wounded in battle, and outraged by the barbarous treatment meted out to them in the name of medicine, he looked for a more humane way of treating their injuries.

At that time firearms were a new weapon, and the method thought most suitable to treat bullet wounds was to pour boiling oil onto them. It caused fearful pain and gross swellings. Paré

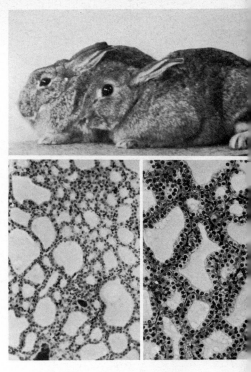

Top: physical changes in a rabbit, caused by stress. The animal with the enlarged eyes (on the right) has been scared by a barking dog. Above: sections of the thyroids of the two rabbits, showing the difference between that of the unfrightened animal and the agitated animal (on the right).

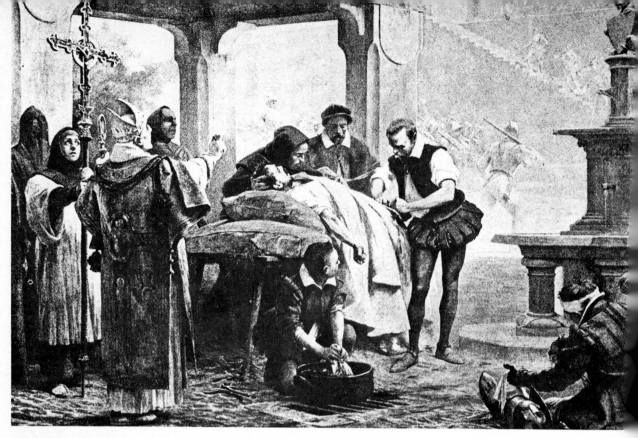

Below: Paracelsus, the 16th-century physician and alchemist. He said that the art of medicine stood on four pillars, the fourth of which—equally as important to the practice of medicine as the others—was love: the healer's genuine concern for his patient.

introduced a soothing ointment that brought relief instead of suffering and caused no swelling. It also healed the wound more rapidly. Paré recommended that there be the sound of gently trickling water or soft music near a sickbed to make the patient feel better. When spirits improved, he said, the body improved.

Paré realized that love is positive therapy. Many spirit healers feel the same. They say that their only way of interpreting the healing power they feel flowing out of them is by thinking of it as the power of love. In his *Revolution in Medicine* the English author Brian Inglis sums up what proponents of many different treatments have said in different ways: "Health lies in an intimate relationship with our capacity to release our real feelings; and in turn is related to our capacity to love. To be able to love is to have health within our reach." It may be that love has a beneficial effect on health because it enables the individual to release repressed energies toward an appropriate object, and thus reduce the individual's accustomed absorption with self. But it may be that love has some other unsuspected or overlooked therapeutic power as well.

Someone sick with scurvy will only recover his health on being supplied with a diet containing Vitamin C. Other ailments require specific remedies too, though very few need as precise a treatment as scurvy. Looking back over the wide variety of treatments available it would seem that a sick person's best course is to follow the treatment that best assists him to cure himself. Different people will find confidence in different systems. Some place their trust in an individual, some in a group, others in the spirits of the dead, and still others in God. The various healing arts are of value insofar as they successfully encourage the sick consciously and unconsciously to heal themselves.

Above: the physician Ambroise Paré, who first treated gunshot wounds with soothing oil. He discovered that patients responded better to his methods of gentle, thoughtful medication.

Right: health is appreciated most poignantly by the sick—and the return to health is increasingly recognized as a process in which the mind and spirit of the patient play a crucial part. Whatever treatment is chosen, it must mobilize the hidden strength of the patient's own will to live.

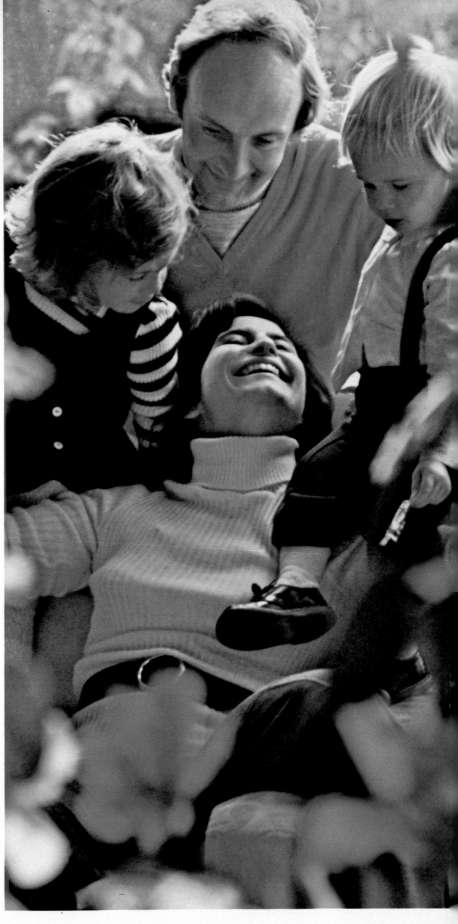

Picture Credits

Key to picture positions: (T) top (C) center (B) bottom; and in combinations, e.g. (TR) top right (BL) bottom left

2   Transworld
4   Musée du Louvre, Paris/Giraudon
7   Bill Eppridge *People* © Time Inc. 1975
9(T)   Musée d'Histoire de la Medicine, Paris/Photo J.-L. Charmet
9(B)   Harry Benson *People* © Time Inc. 1975
10(R)   Bibliothèque de l'Ancienne Faculté de Medicine, Paris/Photo J.-L. Charmet
11(TR)   Bob Peterson *People* © Time Inc. 1975
11(B)   Stanley Tretick *People* © Time Inc. 1975
12(T)   John Olson *People* © Time Inc. 1975
12(B)   Reproduced with the permission of John Weatherhill Inc.
13   Bill Eppridge *People* © Time Inc. 1975
15(T)   Syndication International Ltd., London
15(B)   Camera Press Ltd.
16(T)   Aldus Archives
16(B)   The Bettmann Archive
17(T)   British Museum/Photo John Freeman © Aldus Books
17(B)   *Radio Times* Hulton Picture Library
19(T)   Photo © Aldus Books
19(B)   Photo *Sunday Citizen & Reynolds News*
23   British Museum/Photo John Freeman © Aldus Books
24(L)   Werner Forman Archive
24(R)   Musée des Arts Decoratifs, Paris/Photo J.-L. Charmet
25   E. S. Ross
26(L)   Werner Forman Archive
27   Royal Ontario Museum, Toronto, Canada
28(T)   Michael Holford Library photo
28(B)   Werner Forman Archive
29(T)   Axel Poignant
29(B)   Photo Mauro Pucciarelli, Rome
30(T)   British Museum/Photo John Freeman © Aldus Books
30(B)   British Museum/Photo The Mansell Collection
31   Musée du Louvre, Paris/Giraudon
32(L)   British Museum/Photo John Freeman © Aldus Books
33(L)   The Bettmann Archive
33(R)   Michael Holford Library photo
34   S. Apollinare Nuovo, Ravenna/Scala, Florence
35(L)   Michael Holford Library photo
35(R)   The National Gallery, London
36   Musée des Arts et Traditions Populaires, Paris/Photo J.-L. Charmet
38(B)   MS. Bodley 130, f.84. Bodleian Library, Oxford
39   Bibliothèque Nationale, Paris
40   Aldus Archives
41   Photo Roger Charity/Marshall Cavendish Co. Ltd.
42-3   Transworld
45(T)(BL)   Photos Mauro Pucciarelli, Rome
45(BR)   Musée des Arts Decoratifs, Paris/Photo J.-L. Charmet

47(T)   Staatliche Museen Preussischer Kulturbesitz, Gemäldegalerie, West Berlin
47(B)   Victoria Art Gallery, Bath
48, 49(T)   Ullstein Bilderdienst
49(B)   Ciba Pharmaceutical Company, Summit, New Jersey
50   Photo J.-L. Charmet
51   Ullstein Bilderdienst
52-3   *The Daily Telegraph Colour Library*
54(T)   Photo Patrick Thurston/Marshall Cavendish Co. Ltd.
55   Transworld
56(L)   Galerie Rive Gauche, Paris/Giraudon
56(R)   Mary Evans Picture Library
57   Bibliothèque Nationale, Paris
58   Mary Evans Picture Library
59   Karsh of Ottawa from Camera Press Ltd.
60   Terence Spencer/Colorific!
61   Victoria & Albert Museum, London/Photo Mauro Pucciarelli, Rome
63   S. Angelo in Formis, Caserta/Scala, Florence
64(L)   MS. Liturg. 41, f.147. Bodleian Library, Oxford
65(T)   The National Gallery, London
65(B)   *Sunday Times Magazine*
66(L)   Musée Carnavalet, Paris/Photo J.-L. Charmet
66(R)   By courtesy of the Wellcome Trustees
67   British Museum/Michael Holford Library photo
68   Eglise St. Madeleine, Strasbourg/Giraudon
69(L)   Museo Poldi Pezzoli, Milan/Scala, Florence
69(R)   Bibliothèque des Arts Decoratifs, Paris/Photo J.-L. Charmet
70-1   Photos J.-L. Charmet
72(T)   Transworld
73   Syndication International Ltd., London
74   Photos J.-L. Charmet
75   Mary Evans Picture Library
76(T)   The Bettmann Archive
76(B)   *Radio Times* Hulton Picture Library
77   Popperfoto
79   *Daily Telegraph Colour Library*
81   *Psychic News*
82-3   Photos Dimitri Kasterine © Aldus Books
84   Photo Mike Busselle © Aldus Books
85-6   *Psychic News*
87   Peter Tomkins
88   Reproduced by permission of The Lang Publishing Company, 149 Wendover Road, Aylesbury, Bucks.
89-91   Bruno Elettori © Aldus Books
92   Pedro McGregor, *The Moon and Two Mountains,* Souvenir Press Ltd., London, and *Jesus of the Spirits,* © 1966 by Pedro McGregor and T. Stratton Smith reprinted with permission of Stein and Day, Publishers.
93(TC)(TR)(B)   Photos courtesy Henry K. Puharich, M.D.
94-5   *World in Action*/Granada
97   Bibliothèque des Arts Decoratifs, Paris/Photo J.-L. Charmet
98(T)   Bibliothèque Nationale, Paris/

Photo J.-L. Charmet
98(B)   Ullstein Bilderdienst
99(R)   Bibliothèque Nationale, Paris/Photo J.-L. Charmet
100(T)   Reproduced by permission of the Trustees of the British Museum
100(B)   Aldus Archives
101-3   Gino d'Achille © Aldus Books
104   Mary Evans Picture Library
105(T)   Musée Carnavalet, Paris/Photo J.-L. Charmet
105(B)   Mary Evans Picture Library
106-7(T)   Bibliothèque de l'Ancienne Faculté de Medicine, Paris/Photo J.-L. Charmet
106(B)   Bibliothèque des Arts Decoratifs, Paris/Photo J.-L. Charmet
108(T)   With kind permission of Mrs. E. L. Freud
109(L)   Photo J.-L. Charmet
109(R)   Collection Famille Charcot/Photo J.-L. Charmet
110(T)   Aldus Archives
111   John Drysdale/Camera Press Ltd.
112   Kamera Bild/Camera Press Ltd.
113   Tass/Camera Press Ltd.
115   Photo Mike Busselle © Aldus Books
116   *Radio Times* Hulton Picture Library
117   Picturepoint, London
119(L)   Bibliothèque Nationale, Paris/Photo J.-L. Charmet
119(R)   Abbé Mermet, *Principles and Practice of Radiesthesia,* Watkins Publishing, London, 1975
120-1   © 1924, 1946 *Electronic Medical Digest*
122   Edward Russell, *Report on Radionics,* Neville Spearman Ltd., London, 1973
123   *Psychic News*
124-5   Delawarr Laboratories Limited, Oxford
126(T)   Photo J.-L. Charmet, Paris
127(L)   Bibliothèque des Arts Decoratifs, Paris/Photo J.-L. Charmet
127(R)   Transworld
128(L)   The Bettmann Archive
128(R)   Yugoslavia Film, Beograd
129(R)   Photo Mike Busselle © Aldus Books
131   Kennedy Galleries, Inc.
133(L)   Virginia Woolf, *Flush,* The Hogarth Press Ltd., London, 1933, and Harcourt Brace Jovanich, Inc., New York
134(T)   Bibliothèque de l'Ancienne Faculté de Medicine, Paris/Photo J.-L. Charmet
135(L)   Musée Carnavalet, Paris/Photo J.-L. Charmet
135(R)   Ullstein Bilderdienst
137(T)   Photo Ken Moreman/Marshall Cavendish Co. Ltd.
137(B)   Photo Richard Blight/Marshall Cavendish Co. Ltd.
138   *Radio Times* Hulton Picture Library
140(T)   *Observer*/Camera Press Ltd.
140(B)   A. H. Robins Company, Inc.
141   H. Selye, *Second Annual Report on Stress,* Acta, Inc., Medical Publishers, Montreal, Canada, 1952
142(T)   Photo J.-L. Charmet
142(B)   Bibliothèque Nationale, Paris/Photo J.-L. Charmet
143(R)   John Moss/Colorific!